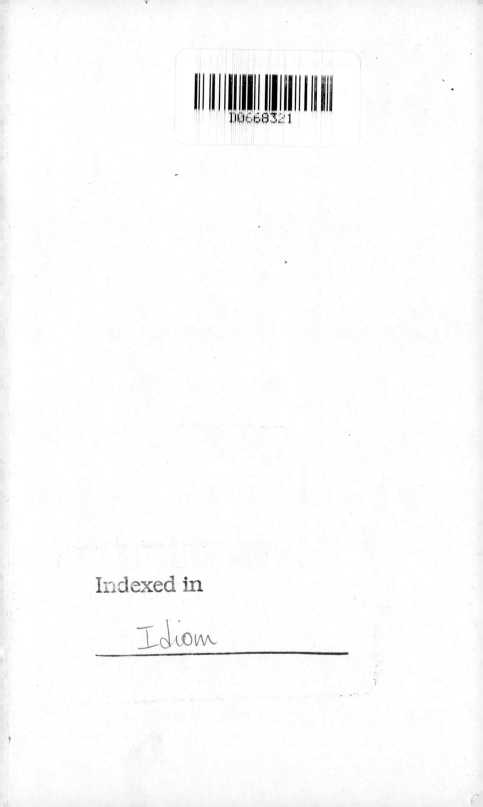
Indexed in

Idiom

Controversies in Sociology
edited by
Professor T. B. Bottomore and
Professor M. J. Mulkay

24
Ideology and
the new social
movements

Controversies in Sociology

Ideology and the new social movements

Alan Scott

London
UNWIN HYMAN
Boston   Sydney   Wellington

Published by the Academic Division of

Unwin Hyman Ltd
15/17 Broadwick Street, London W1V 1FP, UK

Unwin Hyman Inc.,
8 Winchester Place, Winchester, Mass. 01890, USA

Allen & Unwin (Australia) Ltd,
8 Napier Street, North Sydney, NSW 2060, Australia

Allen & Unwin (New Zealand) Ltd in association with the Port
Nicholson Press Ltd, Compusales Building, 75 Ghuznee Street,
Wellington 1, New Zealand

First published in 1990.

British Library Cataloguing in Publication Data
Scott, Alan
Ideology and the new social movements. – (Controversies in
sociology).
1. Social movements
I. Title   II. Series
303.484
ISBN 0-04-301275-2
ISBN 0-04-301276-0 Pbk

Library of Congress Cataloging in Publication Data

Typeset in 10 on 12 point Times by Selectmove Ltd, London
and printed in Great Britain by Billing and Sons Ltd,
London and Worcester.

Contents

Acknowledgements

The following people read parts or all of earlier drafts, and I should like to acknowledge their patience and assistance while absolving them of any responsibility for remaining shortcomings: Tony Jarvis, Brigitte Scott, Patrick LeGalés and Tony Rees. I wish also to thank the editors for their encouragement and for their detailed and highly constructive comments, and particularly Tom Bottomore for his enthusiasm for this project. Finally, thanks are due to the Warden and Fellows of Nuffield College where I was able to pursue my interest in the sociology of social movements.

Introduction

As the eighth of his 'nine theses on the future of sociology' Anthony Giddens asserts that 'social movements will continue to be of prime significance in stimulating the sociological imagination' (1987a, p. 48). This reiterates a view which has become increasingly common among sociologists, namely, that the study of social movements is more than one among other sub-areas of investigation. It is indeed possible to interpret many of the recent, and not so recent, developments within the discipline as a more or less direct response to the activity of social movements. One immediate example is the impact of feminism on the sociology of the family, or on the assessment of class position and social mobility. Perhaps even more radical is the effect social movements have had on the whole direction of theoretical debate in the social sciences, particularly within sociology. The developing concern with cultural crisis in the 1970s both from the Left (for example, Habermas's analysis of motivation crisis) and from neo-conservative or neo-liberal social commentators (for example, Bell's 'cultural contradictions of capitalism') can be viewed as an intellectual assimilation of the implications of the rise of student and other 'new social movements' in the 1960s, or even, more narrowly, as a response to the events of 1968. More recently, the discussion around so-called 'post-Marxism' has been stimulated by the increasing significance of movements which do not display the characteristics of class movements.

Yet paradoxically, the study of social movements has had something of a Cinderella existence. Given that questions of action versus structure and stability versus change have for a much longer period enjoyed centre stage, it is by no means clear that social movements have deserved their marginal status.

The explanation lies in the state of the discipline or, more specifically, in the nature of the successive paradigms which have dominated it.

During the 1950s and much of the 1960s, when functionalism dictated not merely the method but also the appropriate subject of sociological research, the reasons for this marginalizing of social movements were clear. To any theory concerned with stability and functionality social movements were something of a fly in the ointment. They were sources of potential disruption to an entity whose stability, and not instability, was the proper object of analysis. Only by assuming their marginality was the integrity of the theoretical system ensured.

Less clear is why social movements came relatively late to occupy a central place in the Marxist and neo-Marxist perspectives, which gained in significance as functionalism's influence waned. There is of course a sense in which Marxism may be said to be about little else other than social movements, one of its prime concerns being to identify agents of social transformation. But traditionally these agents have been identified as classes, and not as social movements. Class movements were assumed to be *the* paradigm of social movements in general. Actually existing movements were to be judged counter-factually in terms of their proximity, or lack of it, to class movements.

For much orthodox Marxism, social change is thought to occur when an objective location and conscious identity coincide: when social actors become class actors. This implies that there can be only one true social movement within each society, namely, that movement which is also a class one. Non-class movements are viewed critically, and sometimes with contempt or hostility. Writing of the environmental movement which developed in the United States in the early 1970s partially under the influence of Ralph Nader, Manuel Castells, the most influential of neo-Marxist social movements theorists, offers an uncompromising expression of this view:

> In fact, if you think about the implicit content of the themes centred around the environment issue, it becomes apparent that this ideology makes social conflict something natural, by

reducing history to a relationship between Man and Nature, a combination of pre-existing resources . . . The ideology of environment, 'apolitical', humanitarian, universalist and scientific, transforms social inequality into mere physical inconveniences and blends the social classes into one army of Boy Scouts. (Castells, 1978, p. 159).

So, at least in more conventional Marxist analysis, social movements which define themselves without reference to class are a category puzzle, neither fish nor fowl. They have some of the characteristics ascribed to real – that is, class – movements (for example mass mobilization), but they appeal to 'illusory' collective identities such as nation, gender, locality, or even, most disturbing of all, to abstractions such as 'the public' or 'humanity'. The temptation to employ the language of 'false consciousness' in an attempt to explain, or explain away, non-class-based social movements, is one into which much analysis has fallen. Lenin's notion of 'trade union consciousness', or Lukács's distinction between 'empirical' and 'imputed' consciousness are merely the best-known examples of such a move.

Whereas social movements require, as a condition of their existence, a recognition of common interests on the part of social actors, in orthodox analysis classes are defined by objective structural features such as the location of a social group in relations of power or ownership. While the possible number of social movements is limited only by the potential range of collective identities people are willing to adopt (for example, as women, rate payers, animal lovers, inner city dwellers, etc.) a class exists by dint of sets of external definers. In a social movement the actors' adopted collective identity is linked to their understanding of their social situation; in the case of classes, identity is, on the most reductionist view, independent of social knowledge.

Unfortunately, class action tends, at the very least, typically to be mediated by non-class identity. Nation and religion seem to provide a more attractive option for developing the collective identities which enable populations to resist forces of industrialization or colonization. As Ernest Gellner notes, 'conflict will seldom become acute or escalate indefinitely, contrary to Marxist predictions, unless the privileged and others can identify themselves and each other culturally, "ethnically"' (1983, p. 75).

The recent increase of interest in social movements has coincided with a crisis in, or in the case of functionalism the virtual collapse of, such 'single-order' systems of explanation. Increasing awareness of the complexity, of social relations *vis-à-vis* single, coherent, but basically simple, explanatory systems has quite fundamentally altered social theory's conception of its role, and of what it can and cannot be expected to achieve. Sociological 'a priorism' – the assumption that understanding the social world is in the first place dependent on an adequate theory – is giving way to a more humble conception of the capacity of theory in aiding understanding. The mood is again nicely captured by Castells, who himself exemplifies as well as describes this sea change:

> In recent years, theorists in social science – as a healthy reaction against the short-sighted empiricism that forbade thinking about any new phenomenon that could not be measured by some very rudimentary tools – have tried to construct systems of categories and propositions that would enable us to re-code observations in a meaningful, cumulative form. Yet, their theoretical models (from functionalism to structuralism, or from symbolic interactionism to Marxism) have turned out to be as useless as they are sophisticated. (Castells, 1983, p. xvii).

The move away from grand theory manifests itself in a variety of ways, but may be characterized as a shift of emphasis along three axes: (i) from structure to actor; (ii) from static to historical (or synchronic to diachronic) explanation; (iii) from conceptual clarification to theory-informed research.

Precisely because social movements are so problematic for both functionalism and neo-Marxism they receive increased attention during periods of disillusionment with single-order explanations. Growing interest in social action and historical rather than structural analysis, makes social movements a suitable object of research at such times.

The theories which have replaced functionalist and traditional Marxist accounts of social movements have recognized that holistic theories of the social world are untenable in the light of the complexity of the phenomena under consideration. Functionalism, as has been realized for some considerable time, cannot adequately deal with power, conflict or change. But equally the process of simplification of social relations assumed by many Marxist writers has not taken place. Modern societies are marked by greater complexity, rather than less, and the very factors thought to bring about increased simplification – such as the internationalization of the division of labour, increased mechanization – have produced the opposite effect.

I would suggest that there is a double bond between sociology and social movements. On the one hand, sociology's concern with interpreting contemporary society to itself – what Norbert Elias calls sociology's 'retreat into the present' (1988) – places social movements high on the agenda. For some recent social theorists, on the other hand, social movements present a possible solution to intellectual problems, and even a way out of a perceived intellectual crisis within the discipline.

Such a motivation may lie behind all discussions of the 'new social movements', but is most explicit in the works of Alain Touraine for whom sociology *is* the study of social movements. Recent debate has tried to grapple with the implications of the crisis in single-order explanations, and has returned to more detailed examination of actual developments, and accorded the social actor a more central role. As Touraine's work makes clear, social movements are an attractive object of analysis for an approach which wishes to bring the social actor back in.

To pre-empt the argument of this book: in their interpretation of new social movements writers like Castells and Touraine have failed to work through the full implications of this break with single-order theories. The theoretical positions of which they are critical are not merely monolithic, they are also characterized by the desire to ground a normative system in some external, non-normative, and immutable constant: a theory of society, a philosophical anthropology, or science. Although critical of these means, theorists of social movements have remained faithful to the ends of the theories they criticize. One key

motivation of social movement research remains the desire
to identify a single agent who bears, and must bear, the
values implicit in the theory. Not science, not philosophical
anthropology, but an actually existing social agent, in the form
of a social movement, is charged with the responsibility of being
an objective datum for some normative system.

What is meant by social movement? As a rough guide,
I suggest the following definition: A social movement is a
collective actor constituted by individuals who understand
themselves to have common interests and, for at least some
significant part of their social existence, a common identity.
Social movements are distinguished from other collective actors,
such as political parties and pressure groups, in that they have
mass mobilization, or the threat of mobilization, as their prime
source of social sanction, and hence of power. They are
further distinguished from other collectivities, such as voluntary
associations or clubs, in being chiefly concerned to defend or
change society, or the relative position of the group in society.

Such a definition is not novel. In an early work on social
movements Rudolf Heberle defines them with reference to
their aim to 'bring about fundamental changes in the social
order, especially in the basic institutions of property and labour
relationships' (1951, p. 6); I would suggest, though, that social
movements can also aim at defending the social order. Heberle
notes too that the collective action is central in the metaphor
of 'movement' within European languages: 'the connotation in
all these languages is that of a commotion, a stirring among the
people, an unrest, a collective attempt to reach a visualized
goal . . .' (1951, p. 6).

THE ARGUMENT

Chapter 1: In the first chapter I shall outline, in somewhat
ideal-typical manner, the characteristics ascribed to *new* social
movements within recent sociological discussion. The aim of
much of the rest of the book is to question the validity of
these imputed characteristics and the rigid division between
'new' and 'old' movements, but in the first chapter I shall only
be concerned to set out the typical argument.

Chapter 2: With respect to conventional theories of social movements – whether functionalist or neo-Marxist – I argue that their adherence to macro-sociological explanation inhibits an immanent understanding of the stakes involved in social movement activity, and of the specific rationale of social action in this area. *Either* social movement activity is treated as qualitatively distinct from normal or institutionalized action, as in the case of functionalism, and thus implicitly as non-logical or pre-rational, *or* the empirical content of social movement activity is viewed as a manifestation of deeper conflicts, and thus as 'secondary'. In this latter case, which finds its clearest expression in Castells's structuralist Marxism, new social movements are by definition 'reformist', and stand in contra-distinction to 'true', that is, class, movements which, again by definitional fiat, are transformative.

Chapter 3: A more sophisticated second level of reaction to forms of protest as they are actually to be found in Western capitalist societies is to treat them as manifestations of some qualitative shift in the nature of capitalist, or more generally industrial, society. New social movements are thus viewed as symptoms of changes in the boundary conditions of the social system. Unlike functionalist and orthodox Marxist analysis, theories of 'post-industrial' society or 'late capitalism' emphasize the unique and distinctive character of new social movements, but like the earlier theories they remain intent on explaining the development of these movements with reference to social-structural phenomena, in particular social-structural change.

This marks a distinct advance over the earlier theories. Nevertheless, I shall argue that such approaches are inadequate in a number of respects:

(1) *Social movements and social change*: They treat all new social movements as manifestations of the same (general) societal transformation. This presupposes a communality of interests between the movements which is simply not apparent. I shall further argue that the new social movements are not a unified sociological phenomenon which

can be explained with reference to a single set of social-structural changes.

(2) *Social movements and crises*: New social movements are viewed as symptoms of crises within the social system conceived as an integrated whole. Habermas, both in *Legitimation Crisis* and in his subsequent modification of his analysis of modernity (1987), identifies new movements with crises in the cultural sub-system and, in particular, associates them with a posited 'crisis in motivation'. He nevertheless views them as symptoms of a more generalized social malaise which is to be understood in terms of the structural transformation of liberal into late capitalist society. Analysis at this level of generality is not very helpful in identifying either the specific context of the so-called new social movements, nor their empirical aims. While such broad social changes as the rise of the 'new middle class' are important in identifying the social base of new movements, we need, as commentators such as Claus Offe insist, a more specific analysis of the *political* context in which they operate, to identify both their causes and their concrete aims.

(3) *Problems of organization and mobilization*: General theories of societal transformation of the Habermas/Touraine variety fail to examine problems of movement mobilization, organization and issue formation. In Habermas's case this is because he adopts a systems-theory analysis that shifts the focus away from social processes, and although he attempts to link this level of analysis with an understanding of the *Lebenswelt* (life-world) through such concepts as 'inner colonialization', such interpretation is theoretically and methodologically subordinated to explanation at the systems level. In Touraine's case, the matter is somewhat different. Here I argue that his radical social action approach is subverted by intentions which remain historicist and teleological. This induces him to subordinate, once again, the empirical and immanent meaning of social movement activity to a general and logically prior theory of societal development.

Chapter 4: To illustrate the diversity *within* individual 'new social movements', I consider the variety of ideological positions within the West German Green movement, and suggest, contrary to the assumptions of much recent social movement theory, that older ideological divisions, notably that between Left and Right, still characterize ecology.

Chapter 5: In chapter 5 I shall argue that an understanding of organizational and motivational changes is central to an adequate interpretation of social movements, and that the movement/party dilemma illustrates this development most sharply. Despite reservations about its theoretical assumptions, resource mobilization theory offers important insights into these processes. What this theory lacks, as its critics have pointed out, is an understanding of the content of social movement demands, that is, of the 'why' as well as the 'how' (Melucci, 1989, pt 1). This is because of its orientation to a context-independent understanding of mobilization processes and organizational problems. In a sense resource mobilization theory lacks what its rivals have in over-abundance: an explanation of the connection between particular types of social movement and the general conditions obtaining within their social environment.

Chapter 6: Here I shall argue that new social movements can be best explained not with reference to general theories at the macro-level, but rather through middle-range theories: social closure, mobilization and interest articulation. Theories developed within political science should be integrated into sociological analysis.

The critical part of my analysis raises an obvious question or objection: If new social movements are not to be understood in the context of general crises of the system or long-term historical transformation of industrial/capitalist society, then in what social context are they to be understood? The reappearance of protest and social movements in Western societies over the last twenty-five years is to be explained by the failure and inadequacies of the institutions of interest intermediation. In particular, interest groups and especially parties, have failed to respond to popular demands and feed those demands into the political system. Protest and neo-populist movements are a symptom of this failure; they appear in order to articulate concerns and issues which are excluded from mainstream political intermediation and interest negotiation. Thus new social movements are above all political phenomena.

With respect to interest intermediation, the models best capable of dealing with these developments are mainstream political science ones, but they are not narrowly pluralist in character. They have their origins in pluralist, and to a degree functionalist, political analysis, but the socio-political theories to which they are closest are forms of 'neo-pluralism' or 'democratic elitism' of the Weber/Schumpeter variety. While such a view is incompatible with much orthodox Left analysis, as well as with quasi-Utopian notions such as the 'ideal speech situation', there is a growing degree of consensus between Marxist and non-Marxist political sociology in these respects (see especially, Hindess, 1986 and 1987; Hirst, 1986; Laclau and Mouffe, 1985).

Finally, I consider some implications of such a model for the interpretation of the nature and significance of new social movements:

(1) One consequence of the above argument is that new social movements cannot be viewed as a coherent sociological category, they are rather manifestations of 'dysfunctions' in political decision-making processes. The 'unique' socio-logical characteristics imputed to them, such as stress on lifestyle, loose organizational structure, etc., are generaliz-able to social movements as such.

(2) The criteria of social movement success – or their 'effects' – which are implicit in much sociological analysis (for example, survival as an integral entity, transformation of social relations, etc.) are inappropriate. 'Success' takes the form of integrating previously excluded issues and groups into the 'normal' political process. If there is a telos of social movement activity then it is the normalization of previously exotic issues and groups. Success is thus quite compatible with, and indeed overlaps, the disappearance

of the movement as a movement. This argument is diametrically opposed to Touraine's analysis of social movements as pure forms of activity outside the political system.

(3) This argument implies that a crucial factor in the future development of the 'new social movements' will be the reaction of already institutionalized forms of interest intermediation, and above all parties. This reaction will be a decisive determining factor in the development and the potential normalization of the new politics. This again contrasts with macro-level sociological explanation which equates integration with social movement failure.

1

New social movements – major themes

The period since the 1960s has seen the emergence or re-emergence of a wide variety of social movements. Many of the developments to which the label 'new social movements' later became applied were in fact revivals of earlier movements. This is especially so with those whose impact was first felt in the USA: black civil rights and black power, and women's liberation.

The black civil rights movement had its immediate origins in civil rights actions in the southern states in the 1950s, but could look back on a history of resistance to racial inequality reaching back into the nineteenth century (see Marable, 1985).

Similarly, the women's liberation movement could see itself as a revival of previous initiatives to protect and extend women's rights (Banks, 1986). In this spirit both the black movement and the women's movement were concerned to reconstruct the hidden history of blacks or women, and of their struggles against white or male oppression.

It is, however, to the students' movement of the late 1960s that the label 'new' may be most unproblematically applied. The students' movement was more directly a response to specific contemporary events, above all to the war in Vietnam. The imminent prospect of conscription into a distant war, where neither the possibility of quick victory nor a convincing political and moral justification were at hand, led to violent clashes on American university campuses during the summer of 1968. These events hit middle-class Americans in a way in which racial conflicts could not.

While women's liberation, and gay liberation, came via the USA, Western Europe had nevertheless had an active peace movement in the form of anti-nuclear campaigns since the early 1950s. But the immediate accompaniment of the emergence of allegedly new social movements in Europe was the appearance of the students' movement and the events of 1968. Furthermore, the students' movement had many of the characteristics ascribed to new movements generally: except briefly in France, in terms of its composition and aims the students' movement was quite distinct from the workers' movement; its focus of attention broadened out from political issues to those of values and life-styles; it was anti-authoritarian and it resisted incorporation into institutionalized politics.

In this chapter I wish to show how these characteristics are imputed to new social movements generally, indeed, how they are thought to define recent movements and distinguish them categorically from the central movement of industrial society: the workers' movement. The ideal type described here emphasizes the largely cultural character of new social movements, their loose organizational structure, and their emphasis upon life-style, rather than conventionally political, issues.[1] This is a characterization of new social movements the validity of which I shall later question. In the meantime, it is necessary to give an impression of the standard treatment of new social movements within current sociological discussion.

To classify diverse movements under the heading 'new social movements' requires that they have enough in common to be treated as related social phenomena. But what, if anything, do these movements have in common beyond the fact that they are roughly contemporaneous? Can we identify common characteristics within these movements with respect to the types of demands they make, their organizational forms, or their ideologies? Or, alternatively, is it possible to identify broader changes within society to which all new social movements are a reaction?

The distinction implied here between descriptive and structural grounds for treating new social movements together is artificial in the sense that the common empirical characteristics imputed to new social movements are often thought to stem from their shared position within industrial, or post-industrial, society. Nevertheless, the distinction is useful in understanding the debate around new social movements within contemporary sociology and political science.

Within the literature on new social movements we can identify the following types of argument supporting the view that new movements are, at least potentially, a coherent social force, or at least constitute a reaction to some common set of circumstances:

(1) Some studies assume or assert clear empirical similarity between new social movements. This view is also common within literature stemming from the social movements themselves, and arguments to this effect are often made on political grounds.

(2) Social movement theorists, such as Alain Touraine, impute empirical similarities to new social movements on the basis of a broader sociological analysis of contemporary society. For Touraine, new social movements are both bearers and symptoms of the transition from industrial to post-industrial society. Similarly, for Habermas, new movements are to be understood in the context of the long historical process of rationalization within Western societies. As such they develop common themes in criticizing traditional values which have thus far remained unchallenged by processes of rationalization.

(3) Finally, one can argue that, while new social movements are empirically highly heterogeneous, they can nevertheless be treated as a unity because of their social location (for example, within civil society, not the state) and on the basis of their structural similarities. The prominent Italian social movement theorist Alberto Melucci comes close to this view in his analysis of 'social movement sectors'.

I shall return to the theoretical and structural argument in later chapters. Here I wish to draw an ideal-type view of new social movements and discuss its adequacy largely on descriptive grounds. As well as sketching in the kind of phenomena around which debate centres, I shall argue that descriptively we can at best identify a series of 'family resemblances' or elective affinities between these movements. New movements are characterized as much by diversity as by their shared characteristics. Discussion will focus on movements' aims and demands, their ideologies, and their organizational characteristics.

AIMS, IDEOLOGY AND ORGANIZATION

Running together much of the debate about new social movements we can draw an ideal-type picture of the nature of their aims and demands. The following characteristics are most prominent:

(1) New movements are primarily social.

One repeated motif in the discussion of new movements is the view that they are, in contrast to older movements, primarily social or cultural in nature and only secondarily, if at all, political. The workers' movement, according to this argument, was concerned with the question of workers' rights and with gaining access for the working class into the political process through the extension of the franchise, the formation of workers' political parties, the legalization of unions, etc. Thus the history of the workers' movement can be understood in terms of the central social democratic concepts of citizenship and representation. It was the extension of citizenship which was the central aim of the workers' movement and, because the extension of citizenship was a political aim and required political means, the workers' movement is to be understood first and foremost as a political movement. A similar argument can be made for early feminism, given its focus on the issue of franchise, and for earlier black movements.

In contrast, new movements are understood as first and foremost *social* movements. Their concern is less with citizenship, and hence with political power, than with the cultural sphere, their focus being on values and life-styles.[2] Thus 'modern social movements are *primarily social* and *not directly political* in character. Their aim is the mobilization of civil society, not the seizure of power' (Feher & Heller, 1983, pp. 37).

(2) New movements are to be located within civil society.
   Consistent with the above is the view that new social movements 'bypass the state', to use Claus Offe's phrase (1980). New movements are located within civil society and are little concerned to challenge the state directly. Their aim is instead to defend civil society against encroachment from the increasingly technocratic state (Touraine), or from 'inner colonialization' by the society's technocratic substructure (Habermas, 1987). The significance of this concern with civil society has been understood variously as an indication of the breadth of social movement concern – 'contemporary social conflicts are not just political, since they affect the system as a whole' (Melucci, 1984, p. 823) – or, alternatively, as implying the essentially symbolic nature of their activities and ideology:

   In new social movements, the groups . . . accomplish the task of letting individuals re-define symbolic relations between them, with society, with nature, creating other relation networks which radically oppose the 'mass' and its atomization. (Sassoon, 1984, p. 871).

(3) New movements attempt to bring about change through changing values and developing alternative life-styles.
   If it is not through the political system and political action that new movements hope to achieve their effects, then how? In answering this question many theorists of new movements point to the movements' concern with cultural innovation, the creation of new life-styles and the challenge they present to traditional values. The focus on symbols and identities is viewed as the source of the new social movements' significance. Melucci, for example, argues that new social movements can become 'class movements' in the sense of challenging the principles of production and distribution, precisely because of their concentration on identity and symbols, since it is precisely here that modern capitalist production is focused. In contemporary capitalist society productive systems 'no longer concern the sole production of economic resources but also the production

of social relationships, symbols, identities and individual needs' (Melucci, 1981, p. 179).

One central type of identity on which new movements are thought to concentrate is that of the movement's members. Here too we see a shift away from the overtly political: The more individuals develop a sense of personal integrity and autonomy, the more they will interpret changes in the social and political structure in terms of the effects they have on their personal situation, and, accordingly, develop idiosyncratic patterns of interest articulation. (Nedelmann, 1984, p. 1,035).

This distance of social movement from politics has been seen as a condition of its success: 'collective control of development can only be secured by keeping open the space which separates a movement from a decision-making apparatus' (Melucci, 1981, p. 191). Here it is assumed or argued that within new movements the attempt is made to bring about social change through challenging values and the identities of social actors rather than by more conventional and directly political action: 'Underlying this cult of making personal confessions in public is a change in the social definition of what belongs to the private sphere and, therefore, should be kept private, and what belongs to the political sphere and should be made public' (Nedelmann, 1984, p. 1,035).

On the basis of much recent discussion of new movements, we can characterize their aims broadly as bringing about social change through the transformation of values, personal identities and symbols. These movements are identity involving and transforming, they self-consciously manipulate symbols and they challenge entrenched values. This can best be achieved through the creation of alternative life-styles and the discursive re-formation of individual and collective wills.

The characteristics imputed to new movements may be summarized by contrasting them with the workers' movement in a few key areas: the social location, the aims, organizational form and the medium through which they work.

The table of new social movements captures many of their central characteristics: the emphasis on such psycho-social

Table 1.1 Key points of contrast between new movements and the workers' movement:

	Workers' movement	New social movements
Location	increasingly within the polity	civil society
Aims	political integration/ economic rights	changes in values and lifestyle/ defence of civil society
Organization	formal/hierarchical	network/grass roots
Medium of action	political mobilization	direct action/ cultural innovation

practices as consciousness raising, group therapy, etc.; the attempt to create a free social and geographical space for experiments in life-style such as occurs in squatters' movements or in the renovation of urban areas of the type Castells describes among the gay community of San Francisco (Castells, 1983); the emphasis on the political nature of the personal within feminism; the emphasis on grass-roots democracy in ecology, and so on. Nevertheless, the question remains whether we can without distortion interpret the totality of these movements, or at least their central characteristic qualities, in primarily cultural terms.

One way of addressing this question is to examine the terms in which new social movements cast their demands and define their ideologies to see whether there are a few broad concepts which characterize these movements. This is what Feher and Heller have done by identifying new social movements' ideology with freedom and life (1984). Here I shall discuss the new social movements' aims and demands with regard to the notion of autonomy, since this may be a better candidate than freedom in such a general characterization.

There are several aspects of autonomy which new social movement demands may be thought to embody: first, *personal autonomy* is explicitly thematized in several social movements. Psycho-social practices, such as consciousness raising within the women's movement, have had as at least one of their aims the liberation of individual women from personal and ideological barriers to personal freedom through the reconstruction of their life histories and by making them aware of personal oppression, while at the same time stressing their potential power as women. As Sheila Rowbotham observes: 'Within the small group it has been important that every women has space and air for her feelings and ideas to grow' (1979a, p. 40).

Second, many of the more narrowly 'political' aims of new social movements can be understood as an extension of personal and group autonomy by challenging *de jure* or *de facto* restrictions on freedom. Thus arguments for free abortions on demand can be viewed as a way of increasing a woman's freedom to make choices concerning her own body, or the removal of gender or racial discrimination at work as extending the range of individual and collective freedom enjoyed by group members. Social or political rights are relevant here in so far as they increase the sphere of personal autonomy and release the individual from conditions which are oppressive and constraining.

Third, new social movements have demanded what might be referred to as '*autonomy of struggle*', that is, the insistence that the movement and those it represents be allowed to fight their own corner without interference from other movements, and without subordinating their demands to other external priorities.

These aspects of autonomy are closely linked. Within the women's movement, for example, the demand that a woman has the right to develop her personality and think through her politics in a situation free from male influence thematizes both personal autonomy and the autonomy of the movement. Here autonomy, specifically independence from men, is seen as a pre-condition for both the development of human potential, and effective feminist politics.

But to conceive of new social movement aims exclusively in relation to concepts like autonomy can be misleading. The increase in personal autonomy achieved through consciousness raising, for example, has important ideological and political implications over and above the issue of personal freedom. As one commentator of the American women's movement notes:

> The emergence of a mass movement depends on the development of group consciousness. People need to reject old group images for new roles and to understand that the roots of their problems cannot be solved by their individual efforts before they will look to political remedies. This consciousness is learned. (Klein, 1984, p. 81).

This emphasis on autonomy of the subject is thus balanced by an idea of solidarity within the movement, and between members – captured, for example, in the notion of sisterhood. Mutual support both fosters solidarity and defines the movement's boundaries.

The attempt to link personal experience to movement ideology is crucial in this process: 'the link of feminism to daily experience explains why it is a much stronger influence on women's evaluation of their own movement' (Klein, 1984, p. 133). This association of what C. Wright Mills referred to as 'personal troubles' and 'public issues' (1970, p. 14) has been a consistent theme. It can be seen, for example, in the insistence that an individual's politics be translated into his/her personal relations, and in the importance given to the task of creating new images through slogans ('black is beautiful') or substituting new terms for older derogatory or patronizing ones ('gay' for 'homosexual'; 'black' for 'negro', 'woman' for 'girl', etc.). The personal is linked to the political both empirically – oppression shapes interpersonal relations – and morally – political commitment ought to be translated into behavioural changes. This emphasis on interdependence of personal and political has caused some writers on new social movements to speak of 'the end of the separation between public and private areas' (Melucci, 1981, p. 180).

Similarly, what I have called 'autonomy of struggle' has clear political implications. This can be seen most strikingly in attempts to distance the project of particular movements from that of the Left, or occasionally to prevent the hijacking of movement demands by the Left. Both the women's movement and the black movement have, with varying degrees of consistency, insisted on the independence of their concerns from those of the male or white working class: 'I don't believe it is a matter of adding bits to a pre-existing model of an "efficient" "combative" organization through which the working class (duly notified and rounded up at last) will take power' (Rowbotham, 1979, p. 146).

The question of these movements' relationships to the Left has been a contentious one and has opened up a spectrum of opinion. In the women's movement, for example, it ranges from on the one hand those who accept the argument that socialism entails women's emancipation to, on the other, forms of radical feminism which insist on the absolute autonomy of women's struggles. Those adopting a half-way position (socialist feminists and Marxist feminists) have found their ground difficult to maintain in the face of pressures from both sides: male socialists, and radical feminists. The promise, or the hope, of these attempts to accommodate new political demands to traditional socialist politics, results in a new synthesis with wider appeal: 'one reason why socialism has become so sterile and dead to most working class people in the post-war years is because it has not, until recently, become open to the understandings arrived at through the movement of oppressed groups and classes' (Wainwright, 1979, p. 7).

As I have indicated earlier, some theorists of new social movements have been led by the centrality of notions of autonomy, freedom, etc., to define new social movements as primarily orientated to civil society and culture (as opposed to the state, and/or the economic sub-system). Thus they were categorically distinct from older social movements which were concerned with state power – either, as revolutionary parties, wanting to take over the state, or, as social democratic parties, unions, and so on, wanting participation in political and economic decision-making.

There are, however, a number of reasons why notions such as autonomy, or its alternatives ('freedom', 'life', etc.) cannot bear the weight of this type of argument, that is, they cannot act as *differentia specifica* which categorically distinguish new from older movements. In the first place, many demands, even for personal autonomy, are also political demands in a conventional sense. Free abortion on demand, for example, may be couched in the language of autonomy or choice, but it is still a demand on resources, and thus on the state. Other demands, although not in this sense directed at state institutions, nevertheless entail demands which are more narrowly political. No argument concerned with relations within families, for example, can avoid engaging the legal and legislative apparatus which surrounds the institution of the family, for example, divorce laws or taxation regulations.

The point here is that while new movements may be distinguished from older movements because their demands are expressed in terms of autonomy rather than citizenship, etc., such notions themselves entail a whole range of political questions and demands. An attempt to define new movements as essentially concerned with cultural questions is to assume too unambiguous a division between questions of personal/group autonomy and more 'traditional', 'narrow' political issues and demands. The personal is not political merely in the sense that power relations are embedded in personal ones, but also in the sense that demands for personal autonomy, freedom, etc., are political in nature.

Furthermore, some aspects of new social movement ideology are quite clearly concerned with existing political institutions, and can very well be understood in terms of citizenship, representation, and so on. This is especially so with regard to a second class of new social movement aims, namely, those concerned with 'citizens' rights', that is, with acquiring for some section of the population those rights which are ascribed to the average citizen, and from which particular groups are systematically excluded. Commentators such as Melucci who play down questions of citizenship in new social movements do so at the cost of underestimating the continuity of concerns between so-called new social movements and older movements. It may be inadequate to interpret all demands in narrowly political terms (such as universal franchise), since they include legal, economic and personal rights. But what we see here is not a retreat from the political sphere, but an extension of politics to cover a wider range of concerns and social relations. In the context of this wider sense of citizenship, it is no longer possible to separate political issues neatly from other movements' concerns. As one American black civil rights activist, Bayard Rustin, succinctly notes: 'economic reform is a political problem and the only means of achieving this reform, short of resorting to totalitarian means, is through political organization' (1976, pp. 41–2).

Civil rights movements, or those aspects of social movements concerned with civil rights, are clearly orientated towards central political institutions, particularly towards governments and the legal system. They demand a recognition on the part of society to formal and substantive equality for sections of the population, and respect for the rights of members of those sections to equal treatment not as individuals but as *citizens*.

There is a tendency, especially among Left critics of the black movement or the women's movement, to view such demands as merely integrative, or indeed to dismiss them altogether. At its bluntest, the argument here is that if restricted to civil rights issues the movement will fall prey to a process of integration into existing social institutions which will concede enough to blunt its radical edge without altering the essential features of the dominant order. It is simultaneously assumed that traditional socialist politics is broad enough to cover the concerns of non-labour movements. This view has been prevalent among both the extra-parliamentary and, as Elizabeth Meehan reports, the parliamentary Left: 'For some time, a strong strand of opinion existed on the political left that feminism was a conservative diversion from the pursuit of class equality and that women's rights would be a natural by-product of general social transformation' (Meehan, 1985, p. 81). She further notes that with respect to the campaign around the 1970 Equal Pay Act this attitude was 'a hindrance to the espousal by the Labour Party of the cause of women's rights' (1985, p. 57).

In a sense the interpretation of the character of movements demanding equal treatment or civil rights is correct. Less satisfactory is the assumption that lies behind this critique, namely, that such changes do not constitute fundamental social change. The rigidity of the distinction between fundamental change and reform, and the reduction of the latter to 'mere reformism' is unsatisfactory. It presupposes a rigid distinction between total social transformation (whether through revolution or through an instrumental use of existing institutions) and social reform, while equating the latter with incorporation and de-radicalization, and treating total transformation as the only genuine form of social change. On the basis of these assumptions it is thought possible to subordinate the perceived concerns of individual movements to a hierarchy of pre-defined priorities; thus precipitating a confrontation between the movements and their critics around what I have called the 'autonomy of struggle'.

Closely associated with the issue of citizenship is a third sphere of new social movement activity: political access, that is, the integration of groups into processes of political decision-making. Here too new social movements are more conventional in their concerns and aims than many contemporary commentators have allowed.

The development of Green parties, which I shall discuss later, has not only provided activists with a means of articulating demands not conventionally forwarded by existing parties and pressure groups, but has also enabled groups who were under-represented by the major interests (for instance, the young) to increase their political influence.

[The politically integrative function of the new social movements suggests that their development can be seen, in part at least, in more conventionally political terms, namely, as a consequence of the failure of social democratic parties to undergo a process of political renewal.] Particularly within European ecology movements the criticism is often made that social democratic parties have either stuck too closely to the major historical interest they represent, or they have adopted 'statist' strategies thorough which they hope to win wider appeal as effective managers of the Welfare State and mixed economy (for example, in West Germany).

In the view of its critics, social democratic ideology appears increasingly irrelevant to those sections of the public who do not identify themselves primarily as 'workers' and have lost any clear ideological identity. Gransow and Offe have argued for such a case:

> The statist management of social problems, generally cut off from any connection with the experiences, forms of action and values of the social base, becomes inextricably entangled in the problem that it can never be certain whether or not its solutions will be experienced and accepted as such by those affected. (Gransow and Offe, 1982, p. 75).

In contrast, the new social movements have the advantage of proximity to the grass roots. Unlike the 'political culture of social democracy' (Gransow & Offe, 1982), they are able to represent the interests of groups excluded as deviant, or marginal by social democratic parties in their attempts to appeal to 'average', respectable, citizens.

The final feature of new social movement activity I should like to mention is its focus on *limited* or *single issues*. The term 'single-issue movement' does not well describe the activities of new social movements. Rather, these movements tend to be organized around a range of issues linked to a single broad theme – peace, environment, etc. – or a broad interest – women, blacks, etc. The crucial point is, however, that new movements have not been concerned to develop a total politics, or to subsume politics under a single focus. They have identified specific constituencies, or constellations of interest, and have been content to represent them. This has meant that the distinction between social movement and interest group has been particularly blurred in this case. As I shall later argue, this has caused difficulties for those theorists of social movements who wish to treat the distinction between social movement and interest group as a categorical one and who view the ultimate task of social movements as being that of proposing radical alternatives to current social arrangements in their totality, or who speak of a possible 'unification of oppositional movements in the advanced capitalist societies' (Boggs, 1986, p. 57).

A partial exception to this focus on limited issues has been the environmental movement, which has in some cases formed political parties, and has thus had to encounter traditional political issues of social and economic policy. But even here, environmental parties have largely chosen to remain associated with environmental issues, and have assiduously avoided modelling themselves on established parties. In the case of the West German Green Party, for example, this has meant rejecting the '*Volkspartei*' (People's Party) model of the CDU and SPD. Little attempt has been made to offer something for everyone in the effort to gain wider electoral support, and the Green parties of Europe have largely chosen to adhere to their original and clearly defined range of issues. In this sense they remain 'anti-party parties', appealing to specific sections of the population on the basis of specific issues.

How do movements' aims and demands relate to the ideologies which they develop? The first broad ideological theme of the new social movements, and one which is intimately related to the notions of autonomy and civil rights, is their *anti-authoritarianism*: their stress on grass-roots action and suspicion of institutionalized forms of political activity – especially their suspicion of institutionalization of social movements, such as the workers' movement into trade unions, social democratic parties, etc.

Anti-authoritarianism shifts the emphasis towards direct or grass-roots democracy, and away from formal representative democracy. Owing to its oligarchical tendencies, the latter is viewed as a partial, unsatisfactory and incomplete solution to problems of popular participation in political decision-making processes. Representative democracy is distrusted because it weighs power in favour of the representatives who enjoy extensive autonomy, and away from those they represent, who must, by and large, rely on the integrity of those who act in their name and call on their, largely passive, support. This critique of formal democracy is turned not merely upon existing social institutions, but also upon those social movements which have allowed themselves to be drawn into institutionalized politics and have developed large bureaucratic and oligarchical organizational forms in the process.

The anti-authoritarian character of new social movements, and their emphasis on grass-roots democracy becomes especially clear where they begin to form more formal and political organizations. When, in the early stages of the development of an ecology party in West Germany, activists were faced with the necessity to construct organizations with offices and officers, and ultimately to form political lobbies and a party, they were painfully aware of the potential for oligarchy within the organizational, and potentially bureaucratic, instruments which they themselves were creating. This development increased rather than decreased the stress on grass-roots democracy and on the necessity of tight controls from below. These controls took the concrete form of an insistence that officers be rotated. The rotation principle was seen as a pragmatic solution to the problem of the iron law of oligarchy, and the tendency of social movements, once they took a political form as parties and pressure groups, to be pulled in the direction of institutionalized politics. At the same time, there was the fear of professionalization of social movement concerns, and of an increasing distance between the leadership and the grass roots. An ironic distance is maintained, or at least sought, from traditional politics, institutions and organizations.

New social movement ideology is also thought to be characterized by a common 'societal critique'; that is, a common way of defining those features of society of which they are most critical and which they are most concerned to change. Again it is easier to characterize the common elements in this critique negatively: they do not define the object against which they struggle in the manner of the workers' movement, that is as capitalist society. By identifying, in the case of the women's movement: patriarchy; in the case of the Black movement: racism; or, in the case of the ecology movement: industrialism, as the object of their societal critique, new social movements seek a definition of society which is historically and culturally wider than the concept of capitalism. This characteristic is demonstrated with great clarity within sections of the black movement, for example among black Muslims and Rastafarians.

The Rastafarian designation of white Western society as 'Babylon', for example, implies a clear rejection of the reduction of social critique to a critique of capitalism.

The wider definition of the object of social movement critique is paralleled by the definition of the *subject* in whose name the movement acts and articulates its demands. Here again the common denominator is negative: this subject is not a class subject, but is defined across class boundaries (women, gays, blacks, or, most generally, humanity as a whole). Reaction to these features of new social movements can be divided into two broad camps: those who view them as populist movements which have, as yet, failed to identify a concrete (usually thought of as a class) actor likely to bring about social change; and those who see this move towards a broader, more populist, appeal as indicative of a wider social change which includes the decline of class consciousness and action, or even the decline of class itself as a significant political force.

Theorists and commentators who view the existence of new social movements as evidence of the redundancy of Marxist class analysis and as evidence of a post-Marxist politics, stress the decline of class as the primary political force and its replacement by non-class agents. In this vein Carl Boggs argues: 'Social movements can no longer be understood as secondary to class struggle or as tangential expressions of an assumed "primary contradiction"; they have a logic and momentum of their own that needs to be spelled out theoretically' (Boggs, 1986, p. 62).

Those inclined towards this analysis have been concerned to demonstrate that new social movements replace the workers' movement as potential bearers of a new social order. To sustain this argument they must identify common positive characteristics of these movements above all with regard to their societal critique, and the subject they represent. Attempts to demonstrate the plausibility of such a case have come increasingly to focus upon the ecology movement as the one with the widest potential support, and the one most likely to synthesize the disparate concerns of the new social movements into a coherent oppositional force. In other words, there has recently been a tendency within some social theory to ascribe the totalizing capacities traditionally assigned to the working class to the ecology movement. It is argued that technocracy replaces capitalism as the defining institution of society. It is the transcendence of the technocratic society which is then equated with progressive social change.

In this broad characterization of the aims, demands and ideology of new social movements two points emerge. First, although such movements do thematize autonomy and are concerned with questions of values and life-styles, these demands are not discrete from more conventionally conceived political practices while many other demands, particularly those for civil rights, remain political in the usual sense. Second, in their aims and demands new movements are highly diverse. These points raise general definitional questions, and questions about the status of the notion of 'new' social movement, to which I shall later return. Here I shall move on to a further area of possible similarity between movements: their organizational forms.

The organizational form of new social movements is often thought to parallel their ideological project. The main characteristics imputed to new social movement organization may be summarized as follows:

(1) locally based, or centred on small groups;
(2) organized around specific, often local, issues;
(3) characterized by a cycle of social movement activity and mobilization, i.e. vacillation between periods of high and low activity (the latter often taking the form of a disbandment, temporarily or permanently, of the organization);
(4) where the movement constructs organizations which bridge periods of high activity they tend to feature fluid hierarchies and loose systems of authority;
(5) shifting membership and fluctuating numbers.

Given these characteristics, the term 'social network' may be more appropriate than organization. These loose associations are often held together by personal or informational networks: newspapers, information sheets, local radio, etc. At periods of low mobilization the low costs of such loose organizations mean that a few individuals can carry on a minimal level of movement activity. This brings some strategic advantage to the new social movements not open to more traditional formal organizations such as unions and pressure groups: 'because of their non-commitment to stable organizational forms the new political movements are highly adaptable and flexible in response to sudden events and new issues' (Nedelmann, 1984, p. 1,039).

The organizations which most closely conform to the above typology are the local groups organized, often in an *ad hoc* fashion, around single issues. Such groupings are often organized to oppose the local consequences of higher-level political decisions with respect to road building, factory installation, local pollution problems, or, most significantly of all for the development of wider movements, the building of atomic power stations.

A paradigm case is that of the so-called 'citizens' initiatives' (*Bürgeriniativen*) in West Germany which sprang up in the 1970s, filling the vacuum left by the decline of the students' movement. The most striking characteristic of this 'movement' was the multiplicity of individual groups and organizations at a local level. Most remained local and small scale:

> They make an effort to obtain sports-grounds or kindergartens which are not provided locally; they agitate for the building of pedestrian zones; defend themselves against the devastation of inner cities and the raising of bus fares (which have only an economic rationale); or fight against the endangering of the environment through the building of power stations, or the extension of already existing oil refineries. (Mayer-Tasch, 1981, p. 154).

The local- and issue-centredness of new social movements re-inforces the fragmentation of new social movement ideology. Loose organization and a focus on a limited spectrum of issues does not require a high degree of ideological agreement, or agreement on ultimate ends. Thus, new social movements tend, in contrast to more familiar extra-parliamentary political groups, to be characterized by a high degree of tolerance of political and ideological difference rather than by sectarianism. This has worked to the benefit of such movements in enabling them to appeal to broader sections of the population than conventionally and more ideologically unified political groupings. Even where the movements tend towards more formal organization and a broader political orientation, where it becomes more difficult to maintain non-sectarianism, the attempt has been made to retain these features. As I shall later argue, this heterogeneity produces problems in, and limitations to, the development of new social movements into the kind of coherent oppositional force which analysts and some movement members hope or expect.

As we observed in the case of new social movements' orientation towards politics, it is important not to equate them with informal organizations too closely. There is a tendency among analysts, exemplified by the influential work of Piven and Cloward (1977), to build non-formal organizations into the definition of a social movement. In a recent study of the early years (1953–63) of the black civil rights movement in America, Aldon Morris comments upon the highly organized nature of the National Association for the Advancement of Coloured People (NAACP) whose influence on the civil rights movement extended into the 1950s and 1960s:

> The NAACP evolved as a bureaucratic organization. It did not emerge within the black community, nor were black masses involved in shaping the organization at the outset . . .
>
> Decision-making within the NAACP was highly centralized. Most plans of action had to be cleared through the hierarchy in New York. (Morris, 1984, p. 13).

Morris also emphasizes the central role of black churches, themselves closely organized institutions, in the formation of the civil rights movement. He ascribes the tendency to underplay the role of organization as in part the result of a confusion between how the movements are presented and received, and the reality of their activities: 'Social scientists whose accounts emphasize disorganization and spontaneity miss the mark by mistaking an image, projected to and taken up by repressive authorities, for the reality' (Morris, 1984, p. 75).

The degree of formal organization displayed by social movements is likely to be closely connected with the ends they pursue, with civil rights groups displaying a greater degree of organization than groups orientated mainly to personality development. Likewise, ideology is itself a factor influencing organizational forms. While some new social movements, such as the appropriately named 'Spontis' (a colloquial abbreviation for 'spontaneous') in West Berlin, make spontaneity a central organizational and ideological feature, others will be driven towards more formal organization by their wish to tackle higher-level political processes, for example, national decision-making about nuclear power.

Joni Lovenduski's account of the women's movement illustrates this relationship between organizational form, aims and ideologies:

> Women's rights groups have tended to be organized along tractional hierarchical lines with formal structures and clearly stated objectives. Women's liberation groups which are often called 'autonomous feminists' groups, have avoided formal organizational structures, political affiliations and hierarchy. (Lovenduski, 1986, p. 62).

And she goes on to point out:

> Strategically, formal SMOs [social movement organizations] are better suited to short-range goals which involve institutional change in structures whose organizational survival is not the dominant concern. Informal SMOs, with their emphasis on changing people, devote major resources to group maintenance. (ibid., p. 66).

Compared with organizations such as political parties and unions, new social movement organizations are thought to remain relatively loose and informal. This tendency is reinforced by their anti-authoritarian ideology. Where political parties have been formed on the basis of new social movement activity, they have adopted an ironic distance to their own organizational arrangements, and an informal and irreverent posture towards the established norms and rituals of mainstream politics.

Nevertheless, particularly in the case of Green movements in countries such as West Germany and Austria, which I shall discuss later, party organizations have been formed and a parliamentary road has, with some success, been pursued. Those who argue an interpretation of new movement organization which emphasizes informality and the network-like character of organizations may point to the stress even within party-type organizations on grass-roots democracy and on the suspicion of hierarchy demonstrated through principles such as the rotation of offices within the West German Green Party. But here too there is the problem that such principles have been progressively eroded in the course of party development. Furthermore, as Weber has argued, the ideology and grass-roots democracy may do little to lessen the hierarchical nature of movements and parties, but may rather place a disproportional amount of power in the hands of activists at the expense of less active members and supporters. Both problems have been pointed out by Alan Ware who shows that the pressures of institutionalized politics pull parties who are committed to grass-roots democracy away from these principles, in part because of the requirements of efficiency and effectiveness:

> Even those parties (such as socialist ones) which were supposedly committed to some form of control from the base found that the institutional structures they faced were ill-suited to this, and provided little opportunity for the expansion of party activity at the mass level of politics. (Ware, 1986, p. 131).

In sum, it is problematic to use organizational form as a criterion to distinguish new social movements, first, because there is a continuum from loose to tight organization, and second, because there may be a progress within movements towards the more formal and hierarchical end of this continuum.

Thus organizational form raises similar problems for the interpretation of new movements as do their aims and ideologies.

CONCLUSION

In this chapter I have tried to show at the descriptive level that there is both a high degree of diversity among the new movements as to their aims, ideologies and organizational forms, and that there are important continuities between new and older social movements. Thus the claim that new movements are to be understood in a way which is qualitatively different from traditional approaches (for example, those which stress the significance of class and politics) cannot be sustained on empirical grounds alone.

The argument that there is a discontinuity between new and old movements does not, however, rest primarily on an empirical claim. Rather, theorists such as Touraine and Melucci, but also, in a different way, Habermas, point to underlying social changes through which the distinctiveness of new movements can both be identified and explained.

In chapter 3 I shall consider these wider sociological and developmental arguments. But in order to locate more precisely the debate around new movements it may first be useful to discuss the traditional – both functionalist and neo-Marxist – theories because the interpretations of new movements are to be understood, in part at least, as a reaction to the inadequacies of more conventional approaches.

2

General theories of social movements: functionalism and Marxism

Both the major rival paradigms which dominated sociology from the 1950s to the 1980s, functionalism and neo-Marxism,[1] have proffered a general theory of social movements. The methodological and normative starting points of these two paradigms contrast sharply. Functionalist theorists of social movements have adhered to a view of sociological explanation as a form of 'empirical theory' the methodological principles behind which are loosely positivist. That is to say, first, they assume a unity of scientific method, namely, the view that the natural and social sciences share a common structure; second, they equate explanation with universalizable laws, that is, laws which are context independent and which hold across time, space, and, for the social sciences, cultural and historical contexts.

Consistently with their methodological principles, functionalists assume an objectivist attitude towards the phenomena they describe. They would reject the critical theory claim that sociological knowledge is in any way connected to a critique of its object, or that there is a necessary link between forms of explanation and systems of action or praxis. It is not necessary here to go into those arguments which assert that this objectivist conception of explanation necessarily carries a conservative normative baggage,[2] but in this chapter I shall argue that in the specific case of functionalist theories of social movements this is in fact the case.

Functionalism in sociology shares with pluralism in political science a strong bias towards institutionalized social relations.

In equating the legitimate object of explanation with political institutions, in political science, or with social institutions, as in the case of functionalist sociology, instances of action not sanctioned by legitimate institutions become anomalous. Because social movement activity is non-routine action it becomes identified as an exceptional state. Like deviant behaviour, social movement activity is taken to be 'non-institutional' in two distinct senses. First, action is non-institutional in that it is not oriented towards central social institutions (government, the family, etc.), but challenges the legitimacy of those institutions. Second, the notion can have a stronger sense of action not governed by rules and norms, action which is spontaneous, an 'eruption', irrational, etc. The functionalist view of non-routine behaviour, of which social movement activity is an example, slips back and forth between the weaker and the stronger sense of 'non-institutionalized' behaviour.

Whereas organizational action is thought to have a form and a high degree of predictability, social movements are disruptive of a dominant order in which stability is taken, on theoretical if not empirical grounds, to be the norm. In the discussion of functionalist analysis it is the tendency to equate social movements with irrational outbursts which I wish to question.[3]

Both normatively and methodologically neo-Marxism contrasts sharply with functionalism. Given the guiding normative principles of Marxism, explanatory concern is focused chiefly on social transformation, not stability. Perhaps even more significant are the points of methodological dispute between functionalists and structural Marxists. While the latter are also committed to a form of the unity-of-science hypothesis, there is a very basic difference in the way in which that method is viewed. Neo-Marxism ascribes the following characteristics to 'scientific' explanation: (i) there is a categorical distinction to be drawn between 'ideological' and 'scientific' practices; (ii) ideologies take the specific form of an empiricist theory of knowledge: the view that knowledge is possessed by a subject, whether individual or collective, and 'reflects' a reality external to that subject; (iii) the 'epistemological break' which characterizes the irreversible shift from ideology to science consists in the recognition that the 'objects' of explanation are themselves theoretical constructs posited within scientific practice; that is, science is self-referential. Thus, for structuralists, functionalist analysis is ideological not because of the normative baggage, but because of its adherence to a particular conception of knowledge, namely, positivism.

Despite these methodological differences, social movements are accorded a no less anachronistic status within structural Marxism than they were within functionalism, though for rather different reasons. Social movements are defined negatively as not-quite-class-movements. Like institutions in functionalism, class movements in Marxism provide a norm against which other forms of activity are measured; a norm in terms of which other social movements constitute deviant cases.

The assumptions behind this equation of true social movements with class movements are most explicit in Lukács's famous distinction between 'empirical' and 'imputed' consciousness (1971). For Lukács, a class's empirical or 'psychological' consciousness will typically mis-identify class boundaries and interests. Only when class consciousness and social-structural location coincide, can the concomitant objective interests be identified, and significant social change be brought about. This view assumes, first, that class identity is fully independent of the activities and beliefs of the class actors. Class, in other words, is defined exclusively in social-structural terms. Second, it assumes that there is one appropriate ideology for each major class location. Internal disagreements as to the true interests of the class are ascribed to false or incomplete consciousness.

Strictly speaking, neo-Marxists have rejected the Lukácsian view of consciousness as a true or false reflection of social relations as 'essentialist' and 'humanist'. Nevertheless, in reducing social movements to class movements, and in limiting the legitimate range of their activity, some form of the empirical/imputed consciousness distinction remains implicit.

In this chapter I shall address the question, why should two contrasting approaches to sociological explanation produce analyses of specific social phenomena which are in many ways similar? In considering this question, I shall discuss the work of the two leading representatives of these two traditions: Neil Smelser and Manuel Castells respectively. To anticipate my conclusion – I argue that underlying these distinct approaches to sociological explanation is a set of common assumptions which override the differences. In particular both functionalism and structuralism assume a deductivist view of sciences generally, and social-scientific explanation in particular.

FUNCTIONALISM: SMELSER'S THEORY OF COLLECTIVE BEHAVIOUR

The fundamental explanatory category of Smelser's theory of collective behaviour is the concept of 'strain'. He chooses this term, he says, because it implies that neither equilibrium nor disequilibrium are the normal states of the social system. This claim appears somewhat less plausible in the light of his definition of strain as a 'condition of ambiguity as to the adequacy of means for a given end' (1962, p. 51). In assuming a means/ends distinction, and in confining conflict to the realm of means, Smelser assumes a basic consensus underlying potential differences. He has ruled out by definitional fiat the possibility that collective action could be innovative in the sense of being oriented to new values or pointing beyond the boundaries of the social system.

The assumption of a unity of natural and social scientific method, and the assumption that the *raison d'être* of explanation is the discovery of universal laws, has specific implications for Smelser's analysis of social movements. Positivism assumes that concept formation and model building in the social sciences consists of the 'creation of master propositions' (Smelser, 1962, p. 385) which generate lower-level propositions with which we then establish the 'conditions under which the proposition holds' (ibid.). Smelser thus offers a general explanation of collective behaviour which moves from the highest level of abstraction (universal characteristics of social structures) downwards through a series of stages until specific concrete instances of collective behaviour are accounted for. Within this 'value added' model, as Smelser refers to it, each stage, while itself indeterminate, acts as a precondition for the next. Collective behaviour takes place when enough pre-conditions are attained. Thus strain is a necessary but not sufficient condition for collective behaviour. The form such action takes, and indeed whether it arises at all, will depend on the presence of a number of other factors, which he arranges within the explanatory hierarchy. In the case of collective behaviour the specific master proposition is that 'people under strain mobilize to reconstruct social order in the name of a generalized principle belief' (Smelser, 1962, p. 385). The next step is to identify the various kinds of generalized belief (hysteria, wish-fulfilment, hostility, etc.), and the conditions under which people develop and act on such beliefs. When conditions conducive to the development of collective behaviour are present at a higher level of the explanatory hierarchy, they act as pre-conditions for the emergence of collective behaviour at the next stage in a series of knock-on effects. At the bottom of the hierarchy are the phenomena to be explained: individual instances of collective behaviour.

Smelser hopes with the aid of this 'value added' model to analyse the different combinations of determinants in such a way as to 'provide the best possible answer to the explanatory question . . . What determines whether an episode of collective behaviour of *any sort* will occur? What determines whether one type *rather than another* will occur?' (1962, p. 18).

There are a number of methodological and substantive criticisms to be made of Smelser's explanation of social movements activity, the most important of which is the inappropriateness of his conception of scientific method to the social sciences. Even if we suspend possible doubt as to the adequacy of a positivist philosophy of science in general, there remain serious obstacles to identifying 'laws' in the sphere of social life. It is particularly difficult to identify the 'conditions of conduciveness', to adopt Smelser's phrase, without slipping into tautology. The problem can be seen clearly enough in Smelser's own definition of one of the forms of collective behaviour he identifies:

Panic will occur if the appropriate conditions of conduciveness are present, *and* if the appropriate conditions of strain are present, *and* if a hysterical belief develops, *and* if mobilization occurs, *and* if social controls fails to operate. (Smelser, 1962, p. 385).

The statement is tautologous because, while claiming to identify the causal conditions for panic, it actually redefines panic. This tautology stems from a conception of model building which does not allow us to identify the phenomena with which we are concerned with reference to specific contexts and meanings.

The difficulty in identifying laws except as tautologies, and in specifying the causal relations between variables, makes it difficult for functionalism to achieve its primary aim: to develop generalizations which have real explanatory power and are not merely *ad hoc*. Smelser's model, like positivistic sociology generally, finds difficulty in living up to its own standards of scientificity. As one critic notes:

> The explanatory power of the value-added model depends on specifying what are the nomological or causal relations among the many variables that are discriminated . . . Smelser, like so many other mainstream social scientists, has stressed that an adequate theory ought to enable us to derive empirical generalizations from our theoretical assumptions. He acknowledges that one should be able to derive counterfactual statements about what would happen if certain independent variables were altered. But his value-added model does not satisfy this requirement. (Bernstein, 1979, pp. 30–1).

A further major methodological difficulty in identifying sociological laws is the identification of some exogenous variable which can then act as an objective and context-independent datum. To achieve this, Smelser must treat beliefs as the *causes* (or causal pre-conditions) of action. As Smelser notes, generalized beliefs are 'one stage in the total value-added process by which we account for the occurrence of episodes of collective behaviour' (Smelser, 1962, p. 80). This means in effect that specific contexts are again subsumed into the general framework of explanation as generalizable causal factors. On this account beliefs become reflexes appropriate to some given external circumstance.

This is a highly artificial way of describing social relations, or the relationship between belief and social circumstance. We do not first have a social situation with specific features and requirements and then beliefs developing which are 'appropriate' to this situation and its requirements; rather, beliefs are constitutive elements of social circumstances. So, for example, strain does not cause my beliefs, as Smelser assumes; rather the beliefs I have will influence whether or not I see my situation as strained. Similarly, beliefs do not come into being in order that I can act in a certain way (for instance, so that I can 'reduce ambiguity'); my acting in a certain way will be dependent on the beliefs I hold (cf. Winch, 1958).

This has substantive as well as methodological consequences. One of the chief aims of social movements must be to influence the beliefs, and more broadly the perceptions, of social actors in order to make those actors see the 'unsatisfactory' nature of their social conditions. In this sense social movements, if they are to be successful, must act to increase strain, or perceived strain, and not, à la Smelser, to reduce it.

Not only does Smelser's analysis set standards for sociological inquiry which are inappropriate, but these standards, even if attainable, may not necessarily be desirable. An analysis which did succeed in producing general laws from basic propositions, or 'conditions of conduciveness', would be profoundly ahistorical and decontextual. While for a strictly positivist philosophy of science this might be thought to be a sign of success, it is not particularly helpful in understanding certain instances of collective behaviour. Each given example would always be explained by reference to the same set of explanatory propositions. The specific qualities of time and place would be irrelevant to our explanation of, say, the French Revolution of 1789, or the black civil rights movement in the United States in the 1950s and 1960s.

This reduction of events to instances of laws also flattens out the differences between distinct kinds of social phenomena. Thus we see panic, hostile outbursts, etc. treated as responses to the same set of structural pre-conditions. But why should these same pre-conditions give rise to different reactions in different circumstances? Similarly, it is not relevant for Smelser's explanatory purposes who the objects of collective action are. Lynching of blacks in the southern states of America, anti-colonial nationalist struggles in the Third World are treated in substantively the same way, that is, as instances of 'hostile action', 'craze', etc.

Some concession is made to contextual and structural differences in the discussion of 'norm-orientated movements' such as feminism. But here too collective behaviour in the first instance exemplifies some 'generalized belief', and Smelser observes:

> A norm-orientated movement involves elements of panic (flight from existing norms or impending normative change), craze (plunge to establish new means), and hostility (eradication of someone or something responsible for evils). These lower-level components appear, explicitly or implicitly, in the beliefs that accompany norm-oriented movements. (Smelser, 1962, p. 271).

Smelser's marginalizing of social movements has its origins not merely in his method, but also in the values implicit in the analysis. His attitude towards social movements is one of thinly disguised hostility. Even the choice of the term 'collective behaviour', as opposed to the more neutral 'action', carries some derogatory overtones. This evaluation of social movement activity is particularly evident in his assertion that the beliefs associated with collective behaviour are more highly 'generalized' than those of everyday life. Such beliefs must be relatively simple and general in order to 'activate people for participation in episodes of collective behaviour' (Smelser, 1962, p. 80). As a generalization this is probably true, but it is no less true of the beliefs which sustain an adherence to present social conditions. Mobilizing mass support whether for social change or legitimization of current social arrangements requires a degree of simplification, and a limited number of readily understood and repeatable slogans. Smelser's concept of generalized belief amounts to an inversion of the values of a rather simplistic theory of ideology.

The combination of abstract methodology plus political standpoint leads Smelser to believe that collective behaviour requires a qualitatively different form of explanation from normal institutional action. In effect, Smelser explains institutional behaviour in terms of reason for actions, and non-institutional behaviour in causal terms. We read, for example, that labour history contains 'numerous instances of hostile outbursts which erupt shortly after the collapse or threatened collapse of an alternative method of expressing grievances' (1962, p. 238). But we need not invoke general causal hypotheses to explain such phenomena; they can perfectly well be explained in terms of reasons for actions, for example, hostile action arises when other channels of action are cut off, perhaps in an attempt to retain a say in a prematurely truncated process of negotiation. The redundancy of deductive explanation here becomes apparent if we reverse the example: it is hard to imagine that he would feel it necessary to explain that numerous instances of institutionalized negotiation erupt in the absence of a collapse or threatened collapse of normal methods of expressing grievances.

Adopting a deductive model of explanation in which action is explained causally and not in terms of reasons for action precludes functionalism from asking a number of important substantive questions about collective action. First, non-institutional action is treated as irrational, or at least as non-rational. Collective action can only be understood as a reactive phenomenon. The possibility that collective action is ends orientated, that it involves elements of calculation based upon practical reasoning, is excluded a priori within the value-added model. In other words, functionalism fails to explain mobilization.

Second, because social-structural factors become in effect substitutes for reasons, the social system is taken as a given, as the fixed point for our explanation of the deviant case of collective and non-institutionalized action. The common criticism of functionalism, that it cannot produce a theory of social change, applies here, owing to the treatment of non-institutionalized action as qualitatively different from normal processes of social action and negotiation.

Functionalism is in these respects quite distinct as a general social theory from its major rival, neo-Marxism. Yet some of the difficulties the latter encounters are similar to those encountered by functionalism. Using the early work of Castells as my example, I hope to show that these similarities arise by dint of the fact that both are general theories, and that this overrides normative and political differences.

NEO-MARXISM:
CASTELLS'S THEORY OF COLLECTIVE
CONSUMPTION TRADE UNIONISM

Castells's normative starting point is diametrically opposed to Smelser's. Whereas for the latter collective behaviour is an interruption to normal social processes, for Castells it reflects the contradictions endemic within those processes. Smelserian theories of collective behaviour are caught within a systems-integration problematic which Castells equates with 'reformist paternalism' (for example, 1976, p. 147). Castells's aim is to develop a research method which is an alternative to the systems-integration approach, and which provides us with a more adequate theoretical framework for the understanding of social practices.

Before the publication of *The City and the Grassroots* in 1983, Castells adhered to an Althusserian account of 'scientific' or 'theoretical' practices which I briefly characterized at the beginning of this chapter. When combined with one basic substantive commitment, namely, the view that social movements are primarily urban phenomena within contemporary society, these methodological commitments directly affect the manner in which Castells proceeds to explain social movements. Given his conception of scientific method, Castells is committed first to identifying the (theoretical) object of analysis. With respect to urban problems this object is 'urban politics'. The next stage is to break down this object into its components: (i) 'the political' which 'refers to the structures by which a society exercises control over the different instances which constitute it, *thereby* assuring domination of a particular social class' (Castells, 1976, p. 148); (ii) 'politics' conceptualized as power relations; (iii) 'the urban' which refers not to such ideological notions as 'urban culture' or 'urbanism', but to a set of problems about 'the organization of space' and 'the process of collective consumption'. The second of these theoretical objects seems to collapse back into the first since power relations are located in class relations and defined as 'the capacity of one social class to realize its specific objective interests at the expense of others' (p. 148). Nor can Castells intend the distinction to imply a notion of power as a structural category versus power and action, because classes are themselves structural entities and not social actors on his account. However, our main concern here is with the third object of his analysis: the urban.

Urban space is not, of course, any space, it is city space, that is, 'a residential unit of labour power' (ibid). Here Castells identifies the city not as a unit of production (such as the factory, etc.) but as a unit of 'collective consumption' (an 'agglomeration'). As part of this definition Castells includes the thesis that 'the role of the agglomeration as a consumption unit is the same as that of the firm as a production unit' (ibid). This view that contemporary social movements are urban in character stems from Castells's analysis of contemporary capitalism. Whereas in liberal capitalist society the focus of conflict is the factory, and the object of conflict wages, working time, etc., in late capitalist societies conflict comes increasingly to derive from such issues as housing, schooling, health, and so on. In other words the linchpin of conflict between classes exists no longer within the sphere of production, but in the sphere of the reproduction of labour power. Labour is caught in an unequal competition with capital for space and facilities, and this competition is essentially an urban phenomenon. Where this conflict gives rise to a collective response on the side of labour, this takes the form of 'collective consumption trade unionism', that is, action which does not challenge social relations in their entirety, but attempts to win for labour a larger share in collective goods.

It is important to recognize that although Castells discusses practices and social movements which are defined as 'an organized system of actors' (1976, p. 151), he is not referring to social actors in any Weberian sense of individuals acting in context and with reference to meanings. The actors are 'agents, whose most obvious expression is in social classes, [and who] are only the supporters of these structural relations' (p. 150). Thus even though Castells distinguishes an analysis of structures from an analysis of practices, the latter is in effect reducible to the former. This is because his aim 'is not to place events back within a context, but to show the realization of a structural law or set of laws within a social process. This operation is equivalent to the demonstration or proof of a law' (p. 151). The law in question is Althusser's modes of production theory, which attempts to specify which sub-system within a given mode of production will be dominant by identifying its basic determinants. Despite its Marxian language, Castells's model of sociological explanation at this stage is essentially the same as Smelser's.

An instance of the kind of issue that might stimulate a social movement in contemporary capitalist society is competition for urban space between large, for example financial, concerns on the one hand, and on the other resident workers whose homes, schools, and public amenities occupy that space. London's Docklands, or older areas of larger cities such as Berlin and Frankfurt, designated for redevelopment are examples here. Some of these cases have indeed given rise to urban social movements, as with the West German examples or the Covent Garden redevelopment; others, London Docklands among them, have not.

This view of model building is in one vital respect similar to Smelser's in that it too conceives of the process as one of moving down from a high level of generality (a theory of modes of production) to the particular object of research:

[P]reviously discovered laws of the mode of production in question can be applied to the problems concerned; and the problems can be used to discover new laws which can in turn be transported to other domains of reality (social forms) in which the same structures are realized in a different way. (Castells, 1976, p. 152).

At the bottom of this hierarchy is the 'urban system', that is, 'the particular way in which the elements of the economic system are articulated within a unit of collective consumption' (p. 153).

There are two determinants of the urban system: urban planning, which reproduces the social structure of the city; and urban social movements, which are innovative in that they produce a 'qualitatively new effect' either at the level of structure ('a change in the structural law of the dominant system' (p. 151)), or at the level of practices ('a change in the balance of forces in a direction counter to institutionalized social domination' (ibid)).

Castells analyses urban social movements by referring to issues (or 'stakes'); the social basis upon which social movements as a 'social force' rest; and their effects on elements within the urban system or on class relations. It is primarily through their effects, rather than type of organization or demands, that we can identify the nature of a social movement. As one critic of neo-Marxist theories, C.G. Pickvance, points out, defining movements in terms of their effects leads to a strict distinction between reformism and movements that effect social transformation:

> [An] organization where the contradictions involved are purely 'urban' (i.e., concerned with the special unit of the process of reproduction of labour power – e.g.issues such as housing, education and collective facilities) and not linked to the 'political' or 'economic' aspect of class struggle, can at the most be an 'instrument of reform'. (Pickvance, 1976b, p. 200).

Or, as another critic remarks:

> To be effective and politically pertinent within the society as a whole, urban social protest must therefore be assimilated into the working class movement (which for Castells means the Communist Party) (Saunders, 1981, p. 198).

Urban protest movements are thus restricted to what Castells calls 'collective consumption' (in Marxian terminology, conflict focuses on the 'social' rather than individual wage). Their activities are analogous to those of trade unions in that they negotiate for a larger proportion of the total surplus produced without challenging the nature of production itself. For urban social movements this means an interest in participation in rather than control over the planning process.

As a theory of social movements Castells's argument runs into several difficulties. Because Castells shares with Smelser a radically anti-social action approach, he cannot account for the presence or absence of mobilization. In defining the social base exclusively with reference to the structural location of the agents, Castells can at best hope to identify the structural pre-conditions of social movement activity, but in themselves these structural factors are at most necessary conditions for action. Again to quote Pickvance, a sympathetic but trenchant critic of Castells:

> [If] one seeks a detailed understanding of how social bases are transformed into social forces a purely demographical approach is inadequate. Such an understanding requires that attention be paid to the *social structure* of the population, in the social anthropological sense of a system of social relationships. (Pickvance, 1977, p. 176).

As we have seen, social relations in the anthropological sense are excluded as legitimate objects of explanation within the rationalist theory of science to which Castells adheres.

Castells's argument remains bound to a distinction between classes for-themselves and in-themselves. It assumes that a shared position is, eventually, a sufficient condition for mobilization along the lines of that social base. That this does not occur is not taken as evidence of the weakness of the assumption, but as evidence of the partiality of those movements which are other than class-based and which make demands other than production-linked. Castells's concept of collective trade unionism exemplifies this tendency.

Similarly, value orientation is ignored, and because of this the theory fails not only to account for mobilization but also to explain why certain stakes, and not others, become issues. Until one allows that an important determinant of issues is people's perception of what the issues are, it is difficult to see how an emphasis on certain issues comes about. Likewise, one must allow that the activities and nature of protest organizations are an important factor in shaping that perception, rather than define the stakes with reference to structural contradictions alone.

The motive for excluding all subjective elements as influences on group formation and issue selection appears to be the desire to retain basic principles even at the cost of reducing the explanatory value of the theory. In particular, Castells wishes to define the productive sphere as *the* source of contradiction in the social formation. All real conflicts are class conflicts around the issue of the ownership and control of the means of production; collective trade unionism can, by definition, only be a partial manifestation of this conflict.

This is a particularly unhelpful set of presuppositions when it comes to looking at new social movements because these, like urban movements, focus on issues of collective consumption which Castells identifies as reformist, and hence partial. Behind these exclusions are a set of assumptions which are in themselves open to criticism: (i) as already mentioned, contradiction hinges on the sphere of production, and (ii) a reform/transformation dichotomy is presupposed.

With regard to production, the emergence of urban and new social movements suggest the need to expand the concept of production away from a classic manufacturing model to include the production of urban space, leisure, etc., in other words, to include those things Castells categorizes as collective consumption. I shall consider this suggestion in the next chapter. Here I merely wish to point out that with his assumptions it is not open to Castells to make such a move since it would dissolve the production/consumption model, and with it the identification of the urban as a unit of consumption, and of urban movements as consequently partial.

The second dichotomy (reform/transformation) results in Castells's insistence that all conflict is to be understood in terms of a classical class model. It excludes a priori the possibility that reforms can be transformative, or that planning or existing authorities (such as local government) can be innovatory:

[It] is taken as axiomatic within this approach that authorities will not grant changes which threaten the stability of the mode of production. But . . . purely urban social movements are not considered to be capable of provoking changes of this scale and the empirical studies bear this out. It appears to me that a different theoretical assumption is being made, namely, that 'authorities' will not grant concessions *of any scale* without the intervention of social movements. (Pickvance, 1976b, p. 203).

If Pickvance's criticisms are acceptable, the most basic distinctions between Marxism and structuralist Marxism would be called into question. Just as Smelser assumes that the social system will always act to stabilize itself, so Castells assumes a more or less smooth-running operation of the ideological and state apparatus which is itself defined in terms of its function in maintaining class relations (see Saunders, 1981).

THE LIMITS OF A GENERAL THEORY
OF SOCIAL MOVEMENTS

The limitations of general theories of social movements, or of other social phenomena, stem precisely from their generalizing ambitions. In order to attain the level of generality towards which they aspire they must exclude a priori many of the most interesting questions raised by the existence of social movements. In particular, they must ignore all those questions relating to social agents and the specific context of their actions. They do not address such questions as: (i) Why does mobilization occur? (ii) Why does it take the specific form it does?

Both functionalism and Marxism are *general deductivist* theories which hope to deduce an understanding of specific events from a higher level theory. Both treat the social structure as a coherent, holistic and relatively unambiguous entity, however strained or ridden with contradictions.

The limitation of such general deductivist theories of social movements, whether functionalist or neo-Marxist, is that they must restrict themselves to identifying the structural preconditions for social movement activity. But the problem is that these pre-conditions are precisely that: at most necessary but not sufficient conditions for mobilization. It does not follow that in the presence of all specific pre-conditions social movements will actually appear, or that agents will be inspired to act collectively. The appearance or otherwise of such movements will depend upon a host of other factors which are context specific, and cannot be deduced from social-structural conditions: the presence or absence of emotive issues or of potential leading actors, the reaction of the authorities, social agents' calculations of the possible benefits of action versus inaction, etc.

There is simply not room within the parameters of general theories for a consideration of these factors. Agents are either treated as fundamentally irrational, or at least non-rational; or their actions only become relevant when they coincide with courses of action thought appropriate given a specific theoretical understanding of the social structure, class relations, material relations, and so on.

In contrast to the theories considered in this chapter, theorists of new social movements have reacted against such universalist interpretations. There has been a return to actual conditions under which social movement activity takes place. No attempt has been made to subordinate social movement activity to pre-given, usually class, interests, and a conscious effort has been made to make sense of new social movements as rational reactions to the conditions prevalent in late capitalist society. Correspondingly the societal critique stemming from within the movements themselves is taken seriously, and not merely treated as a symptom of deeper, but dimly recognized, discontents.

It has been the strength of debates centred around the new social movements that they have moved away from the structural determinism of functionalist analysis, and have turned attention once more on to the context of social movement activity. The question I wish to address in the following chapter is how far this development has gone in reasserting the centrality of the social agent. I shall argue that despite these advances the sociological discussions of new movements have been haunted by the desire to find a direct substitute for the structural category of class.

3
Sociological responses to the rise of new social movements

Let us free ourselves from the heritage of the philosophy of history and think of social systems as the product of collective action.

(Alberto Melucci, 1981, p. 192)

Comparing the American and European working class in a lecture first given in 1967, Herbert Marcuse commented:

What we can say of the American working class is that in their great majority the workers are integrated into the system and do not want a *radical* transformation, we probably cannot or not yet say of the European working class. (Marcuse, 1970, p. 85).[1]

Were Marcuse's exemption of the European working class from this judgement less obviously half-hearted, his comments would be inconsistent with his general views on the nature of advanced capitalism. His arguments at this time illustrate the most fundamental grounds for a shift of emphasis within neo-Marxism from the working class to new social movements, namely, growing uncertainty that the working class will fulfil the role of revolutionary subject ascribed to it.

In Marcuse's view, capitalism had created the material (that is, technical) conditions for liberation. What remained was 'surplus repression' in two forms: first, exploitation of the populations of the Third World, and of underprivileged sections of affluent societies; second, exploitation of the affluent through the creation of false needs (and the associated suppression of real needs) which it then 'satisfied' through consumption. The working class belongs, at least in the United States, not to the first category but to the second; but even here it does not play the leading role. It is among still more privileged groups, for example students, that the experience of the second (cultural and psychological) aspect of capitalist exploitation is at its sharpest, and it is they who are consequently most likely to form a vanguard. It is difficult, in the light of this, to sustain Marcuse's claim that he did not imply the direct substitution of the working class with 'minority' groups or the new middle classes as would-be revolutionary subjects.[2]

The notion that capitalism had overcome problems of economic cycles and recession is one which may now seem somewhat quaint, but the economic and political conditions of the late 1960s seemed to confirm this judgement. This is especially the case with the events of 1968 themselves. What appeared to many at the time classical revolutionary activity was led not by workers but by relatively privileged sections of the population. At the same time, the most active and radical social movements within the advanced capitalist societies during the 1960s were non-class-based in their social base and in their politico-economic demands: the black power movement and the women's movement.

Marcuse's argument, for all that it now appears in many ways a product of its time, captures the essential features of those theories which claim to identify a fundamental shift in the nature of capitalist society, and which consequently place new social movements at the centre of their account of social change. In this sense, theories of new social movements on the Left can still be viewed as a reaction to the events of the late 1960s.

In particular those aspects of the women's movement to which Marcuse drew attention towards the end of his life are still seen by theorists and activists alike as the salient features of new social movements. The women's movement in the 1960s thematized many of the features of a non-class-based political programme. Especially important in this context was the attempt to politicize personal relations, as illustrated by the slogan 'the personal is the political'. The psychological and personal nature of repression, and the consequent need for changes in attitudes as a pre-condition for social and political change became a focus of attention. This theme was picked up and generalized by the New Left:

> *Der Spiegel*: Do you mean that the student movement offers a real possibility of a change in consciousness?
> *Marcuse*: Yes, a change in consciousness and sensibility which is today a pre-condition of radical social change. (Marcuse, 1969, p. 103).

Marcuse's writings in the 1960s pick out the issues which have continued to trouble new social movement theorists who on many specific points, or in their general orientations, would not wish to associate themselves with Marcuse's views. Much of the discussion of new movements is a response to three failed predictions in particular which had left a problematic heritage for those wishing to develop Marx's analysis of class. Giddens has identified these succinctly:

> (a) the disappearance of those classes and segments of classes which 'complicate' the main dichotomous class system of capital and wage-labour; (b) the progressive elimination of diversified sectors within the working class itself; (c) the growing disparity between the material wealth of capital and wage-labour. (Giddens, 1973, p. 35).

Rather than simplifying class relations, capitalism has given rise to diversification of classes, and to the growing importance of 'non-productive' labour (see, for example, Lash and Urry, 1987). At the same time, the proletariat, in the narrow sense of productive labour power, has shrunk.

With respect to the second assumption, the working class remains diversified in any number of ways: politically, ethnically, regionally, by economic sector, etc. These divisions within the working class have been increased, rather than reduced, by the progressive internationalization of capitalism. Finally, at least some workers in core industries in Western societies have been able to protect themselves from processes of wealth polarization, and have continued to secure their economic and welfare position.

The development of a revolutionary class consciousness, which on cruder materialistic interpretations is seen as the necessary consequence of the structural changes initially predicted, has likewise largely failed to appear. Working-class organizations have by and large restricted their activities to demands for improvements in wages, conditions and the social wage without calling the labour-capital relationship itself into question. The degree to which national working classes are radical or quiescent remains influenced by national and cultural factors, (see Gallie, 1983). Where the labour movement has produced political parties these have tended to take the form of left-of-centre social democratic parties whose commitment to abolition of private ownership of the means of production has become a formality (for example, the British Labour Party), or has been abandoned altogether (as in the case of the West German SPD's Godesberg programme of 1959). Likewise, where trade union activity has been orientated to state power it has, more often than not, been in the role of a partner in neo-corporatist bargaining arrangements.

Marcuse's response, the desire to substitute disparate movements for the working class, represents a first line of defence. It is a response which in many ways retains problematic features of traditional Marxist thought while incorporating a new, and no less problematic, philosophical anthropology.

In the first place the argument that the problems of advanced capitalism are ones of surplus repression implies technological determinism by reducing social relations to technical ones, and implying a highly consensual and homogeneous model of advanced capitalism.[3] The possibility of conflict along the lines identified by Marx (between labour and capital) is ruled out, a priori, by the notion of capitalism as a total system in which both the creation and the satisfaction of false needs takes place smoothly. In rejecting cataclysmic theories of working-class revolution, Marcuse replaces the model with its opposite: a picture of complete consensus between the key actors (the state, capital and labour) and conflict at the periphery. But the historical and sociological evidence would not suggest the truth of either of these positions.

Marcuse's category of 'surplus repression' implies a view of human nature which entails a specific social psychology of 'real needs'. His adherence to a substantive theory of human nature, Freudian psychoanalysis, compels him to what might be called a 'naturalistic'[4] solution to the classical problem of critical theory. The rationality of the criteria against which existing societies are to be judged is vindicated with reference to nature in the form of given individual and collective needs. On the basis of this social psychology of real needs Marcuse feels able to assert:

> What they [humans] really want is not unending and eternally unsatisfactory change, not striving for what is endlessly higher and unattained, but rather a balance, a stabilization and reproduction of conditions within which all needs can be gratified and new wants only appear if their pleasurable gratification is also possible. (Marcuse, 1970, p. 41).

Freud is more consistent than Marcuse in recognizing the asocial nature of such a naturalistic critique of civilization. Unlike Marcuse, Freud consistently aims his criticisms at civilization itself, and not merely at one of its forms.

On a naturalistic view, real needs are not those needs which, after a process of reflection or discussion, people feel themselves to have, rather they are biologically given needs of which, with sufficient repression, we may be unaware. This aspect of Marcuse's revision of Marxism can again be illustrated with reference to his attitude towards the women's movement. In his view the emancipatory potential of feminism lay in its ability to substitute qualities of support and caring previously restricted to the domestic sphere and women's roles for repressive relations of power and domination. In this he opened himself to two lines of criticism; from the Left that he was ignoring class, and from feminists that he reified exactly those features of women's lives which were themselves the outcome of patriarchy.

There is, however, a quite different criticism to be made here, one which Alasdair MacIntyre (1970) makes with some force. Because Marcuse's concept of real needs is non-discursive,

naturalistic ethics are open to the criticism that they are
authoritarian: why should we take Marcuse's word for it that
the needs he identifies are our needs, even though he does,
after all, live under the same conditions of repressive tolerance
as ourselves?

I have spent some time on the discussion of Marcuse's now
somewhat unfashionable views because, first, I wish to argue
that some of the motivations and assumptions explicit in his
work remain implicit in the work of later social movements
theorists; and second, I shall argue in the next chapter that
what I have called Marcuse's 'naturalistic ethics' form a central
theme of new social movement ideologists. Now I wish to
consider those later theorists of 'post-industrial society' who
have developed accounts of new social movements marked, at
least apparently, by greater sophistication.

THE POST-INDUSTRIAL SOCIETY ARGUMENT

Although in some respects Marcuse's break with Marxism is,
despite his own theoretical and political commitments, dramatic,
in other respects the task of working through the implications of
rejecting the working class as revolutionary subject has been left
to later neo-Marxist, and post-Marxist theorists of new social
movements; for them the question becomes 'whither class?'

The shift of emphasis away from the working class and from
class itself as a useful explanatory category is a response
to an old problem with the notion of class as an objective
category; this, nevertheless, is said to exercise an influence
over actors' perceptions and actions. This problem, recognized
clearly enough by Weber, has more recently led some neo-
Marxist thinkers, among whom theorists of social movements
have played a pioneering role, to abandon the distinction
between a class-in-itself and a class-for-itself. They treat as
classes only those groups who consciously recognize common
interests and act, at least in certain respects, as a single coherent
entity. In other words, social movements are substituted for, or
equated with, class.

These general theoretical propositions have specific implications for the study of social movements, namely, a shift of

emphasis towards a context-specific analysis of processes and action, and to the content of social movement demands.

It is above all in the work of Alain Touraine that we see these principles examined and applied to contemporary social movements. Touraine's break with conventional class analysis takes place at a methodological level: he adopts a radical form of social action theory which relinquishes class as a structural category. His concern is not with structures as a datum of sociological explanation, but with the social subject as active perpetuator and, crucially, creator of social relations. His first key sociological category is that of 'action' which is defined as *'the behaviour of an actor guided by cultural orientations and set within social relations defined by an unequal connection with the social control of these orientations'* (Touraine, 1981, p. 61).

Touraine has constantly repeated his opposition to theories of social life, whether functionalist or Marxist, which reduce action to structure or to relations of pure domination. This is particularly clear in his critique of notions of class rule, dominant ideology, etc. In order to bring out this contrast, it may be useful to compare Touraine's views with central tenets of Marxist class analysis:

— It is possible to identify long-term developments on the basis of an understanding of the dynamics of the capitalist mode of production.

Touraine: *'A sociology of action should first of all refuse to seek for the natural laws of a social system, since the system is no more than the product of social relations and, at the same time, of history.'* (1981, p. 58).

— The workers' movement has a central role in the transformation of capitalism *by dint of its structural location* within that society.

Touraine: *'There can be no class without class consciousness.'* (1981, p. 68).

— It is possible to identify a priori the objective interest of those classes which challenge the dominant order on the basis of which we can assert that communism will be the aim of working-class movements in the absence of false consciousness.

Touraine: 'The historical actors are determined as much by a cultural field as by a social conflict.' (1981, p. 66).

In a manner reminiscent of Hegel's discussion of the master/ slave relationship, Touraine argues that in human relations, no matter how unequal, there is necessarily an element of mutual dependence and recognition between subjects occupying the subordinate and dominant positions. No one stands outside or above the social sphere, each is involved in a struggle for recognition and control within it. Touraine is consequently keen to stress that societies are 'self-produced' in a process in which subjects struggle for control over the historical context within which they are located. But the self-produced character of society is itself a historical fact: it is in the advanced post-industrial societies in which agents act with the greatest degree of self-awareness and reflexivity. We shall come back to the notion of post-industrial society later; here I wish to characterize Touraine's analysis of social movements.

The dramatis personae in this social drama are collective rather than individual actors. Thus social movements are assured of their theoretical centrality. Consistent with these presuppositions, social movements are defined as '*the organized collective behaviour of a class actor struggling against his class adversary for the social control of historicity in a concrete community*' (Touraine, 1981, p. 77).[5] 'Historicity' is the second key concept in Touraine's pantheon. It refers not merely to historical time, but to the processes of social continuity and transformation which are co-determinate with social action.

In addition to these methodological grounds for placing social movements at the centre of sociological analysis, Touraine offers a number of more substantive considerations:

A society is formed by two opposing movements: one which changes historicity into *organization*, to the point of transforming it into *order* and power, and another which breaks down this order so as to rediscover the orientations and conflicts through *cultural innovation* and through *social movement*. (Touraine, 1981, p. 31).

It follows that if we are to understand social processes we must understand the forces which brought them about and identify those movements which will further transform them. Structural analyses, such as functionalism, are restricted in scope, only being able to explain those processes already fossilized by the successful attempts of dominant groups to defend their gains.

Touraine's rejection of functionalism, including the implicit functionalism of much Marxism, places him in an advantageous position when it comes to working through a theory of social movements that pays close attention to the specific self-understanding of the movements, and the context within which they operate. His methodology of 'sociological intervention' reinforces this. Touraine rejects objectivist approaches to sociological investigation. For him, the researcher must engage activists in a critical discourse which challenges the assumptions with which the activist works, but which aims at the same time to raise his/her action to a 'higher level of struggle'.

How do these general theoretical and methodological principles affect Touraine's analysis of particular social movements? Here I shall briefly consider his analysis of the French anti-nuclear movement (1983a) and of Poland's Solidarity movement (1983b).

Touraine is clear that the anti-nuclear movement starts out as a defensive reaction motivated by fear of accident and ecological disaster. Were it to remain so, however, the movement would retain its localized character, and tend to dissolve itself at local level each time a particular nuclear power station was either built, or successfully opposed. In order to attain the status of a full social movement as Touraine defines it, the anti-nuclear movement would have to (i) clearly define a social group in whose interest it fights – mere fear of catastrophe is too abstract in appealing to humanity as a whole; (ii) define an enemy with whom it engages; (iii) develop an alternative, but not regressive, model of modernity to the technocratic one on offer.

Touraine notes that while the leadership of the French anti-nuclear movement – the militants – have their roots in the May movement of 1968, the immediate stimulus for the movement was the reaction to the accelerated programme of nuclear energy expansion adopted by the French government in the early to mid-1970s. He observes that on the basis of local protest anti-nuclear demonstrations 'became rallying points for all sorts of protests' (1983a, p. 22). Despite the centrality of the issue, and the resonances it found in generalized discontent with modern technology, the story of the French ecology movement, of which the anti-nuclear movement formed the core, was ultimately one of failure. The movement collapsed after its attempt to stand at the general election in 1978 had failed:

> The warnings of some and the last minute withdrawals of others did not change the main fact: the ecologists were going into the election battle as no more than a current of opinion, formed on a theme of central importance and around a general sensibility, but offering no real choice to an electorate which knew that the great confrontation of Right and Left would have a profound consequence for the future of society. (Touraine *et al.*, 1983a, pp. 27–8).

Touraine's task is to explain why this movement failed to develop into a 'class' movement in his sense, that is, a movement which identifies a social group in whose interests it acts, and an enemy. He does so by referring to the debates within the movement which determine whether it would be transformed into a full social movement, or whether it would remain stuck at a pre-social – perhaps purely moral, level of critique, and act only locally and sporadically. To do this Touraine examines these internal debates in minute detail.

At the most general level, the anti-nuclear movement represents a break with the values of both capital and the workers' movement. Unlike, for example, the French Communist Party, it abandons economic growth models and a faith in science and technology. The anti-nuclear movement, like the ecological movements in general, can be located at a point of crisis within both post-industrial society and science. But in trying to work out the exact nature of this critique of a technology the French anti-nuclear movement ran into difficulties. 'But the anti-nuclear militants were unable to show that, in the presence of the representatives of the nuclear industry, they could go beyond a global protest, offer a more precise criticism and define other modes of development.' (Touraine *et al.*, 1983a, p. 40).

In the meetings of the ecologists and representatives of the French nuclear industry which Touraine recounts, the weaknesses of the movement become apparent: 'the strength of the Anti-Nuclear action was not to be found where it appears first and most vividly: in the denunciation of a technology and an industry' (ibid., p. 44).

These meetings were a turning-point. Unable to act as a 'social force', the groups turned in on themselves invoking 'the warmth of communal life, the idea of a richer, more convivial life' (ibid., p. 46). Although the anti-nuclear movement never fully withdrew into this communal Utopia, it nevertheless remained unable to specify accurately the field of conflict – for Touraine, the technocracy – or a specific class adversary.

In many ways Touraine's analysis of Solidarity in Poland can be understood as the search for a movement which contrasts with the anti-nuclear movement in France, that is, a movement which attains a higher level of struggle by identifying a public, and creating an alternative sphere – a society within a society – which reasserts civil society against, in this case, an authoritarian state. Unlike the anti-nuclear movement, Solidarity avoids both dangers of social movement development: retreating into communal Utopias, and orienting itself exclusively towards the state in an attempt to capture state power. As such, it provides Touraine with an example of a truly social movement, one concerned to create democratic freedoms within civil society, and indeed establish that civil society against the background of a totalitarian state. 'The national movement represents the desire to separate society from the state, to restore their freedom to the citizens, to allow them to choose, and to have control over, their representatives, and to inform and organize themselves as they wish' (Touraine *et al.*, 1983b, p. 49).

On Touraine's account Solidarity is both a trade union and a nationalist and popular-democratic movement whose success can be traced back in large part to its 'self-limiting' character, that is, its recognition of the government's right to rule under conditions where the latter's room for manoeuvre was severely limited by the threat of Soviet intervention.

Implicit in Touraine's analysis of the contrasting cases of France and Poland are a set of criteria by which he distinguishes 'true social movements' from political parties, pressure groups, or revolutionary groupings. Some of these have already been mentioned – identification of a subject, of stakes, etc. – but beyond these are further criteria which have their roots in, and are justified with reference to, Touraine's understanding of the nature of modern society.

Touraine's project remains the identification of that social movement *most appropriate* to post-industrial society. The shift from industrial to post-industrial society is marked primarily by a shift in the nature of production away from manufacture-based and towards knowledge-based industry. Associated with this development is displacement of conflict away from the work-place, and a replacement of workers with more nebulous social groupings ('the public', 'consumers') as the prime actors within potential oppositional forces. Similarly, it is no longer the ownership and control of the means of manufacturing production, but ownership and control of knowledge production which forms the main source of social power. Above all, it is the technocratic state against which social movement activity is directed. But Touraine also wants to distinguish true social movements from revolutionary groupings who pose a potential threat to their activities by imposing a narrow and essentially outdated aim, namely, taking over state power. In contrast to revolutionary groups, the social movements of the post-industrial era are primarily concerned with defending and extending civil society against a potentially all consuming state.

Thus the social movements within post-industrial society must neither withdraw into Utopia, nor must they simply aim at acquiring state power. To do either would mean loosing the specific qualities of a social movement.

In closing off the range of legitimate social movement activity Tourainean analysis reintroduces some form of the empirical/ imputed consciousness distinction; that is to say, it sets up criteria for 'ideal' social movements. This is particularly clear in the work of the Italian social movement theorist and one-time Touraine pupil, Alberto Melucci. Like Touraine, Melucci distinguishes class movements from other forms of collective action, such as protest and deviance. Thus 'class organizational movements' operate 'when the collective action within an organization not only goes beyond the limits of the organization and contests its norms but also attacks the source of power itself' (Melucci, 1980, p. 204); and 'class political movements' are 'collective action which not only aims to enlarge political participation, but which also directly challenges the hegemony of the dominant political force and their link with class interests' (ibid.).

The assumptions behind the notion of class movements now become clear: class movements are those forms of collective action which challenge social relations within particular spheres in their totality; demands become generalized to a degree where their specificity is transcended, and the legitimacy of the authorities against whom those initial demands were directed is itself called into question. In this spirit Melucci argues that within class movements the stakes take on an increasingly symbolic character, and become decreasingly negotiable within what eventually becomes a zero-sum game (cf. Melucci, 1980, p. 207).

In subsequent chapters I wish to make two substantive arguments against this model of social movements: first, that social movements are so diverse in their ideologies and the nature of their demands that there is little realistic possibility that they will form a single coherent oppositional force; second, that social movement activity is unstable to the extent that there is no effective third course between sporadic action around specific questions and formal political organization. Here I shall confine myself to more general criticisms of the Touraine/Melucci model.

The Tourainean theory of social movements is highly suggestive. In particular his emphasis on the self-productive nature of movements, and of social relations in general, provides one of the most powerful critiques of theories of structural determination. However, as may already be apparent from the above account, there is an unresolved tension in his argument. On one end, social movements are conceptualized as open-ended, self-sustaining and innovative entities; on the other is a theory of social periodization which limits the possible range of social movement activity, and which forecloses a priori certain developments. Touraine occasionally makes this limitation on possible social movements activity quite clear, as when he asserts 'there is only one social movement for each class in each type of society' (Touraine et al., 1983a, p. 4).

There are a number of difficulties with this conceptualization of new social movements. In the first place Touraine's explanation of the success or failure of social movements is highly movement-centred and focuses too exclusively on ideology at the expense of both organization and the specific political context. Movement organization is the absent centre of Touraine's analysis. Reading his account of the anti-nuclear movements one gains the impression that if the groups concerned were to achieve an adequate self-understanding of their own programme, and accurately identify their opponent, mobilization would more or less spontaneously follow. In a word, his criteria of social movement success or failure are exclusively ideological.

The problematic position of organization within Touraine's analysis stems, first, from his stress on social action (as opposed to organization), and, second, from his understanding of post-industrial society, which precludes much consideration of state institutions. In viewing new social movements as first and foremost concerned with civil society, Touraine has little interest in the pragmatic political issues such as the response of political parties to social movement demands, the relative openness or closedness of the political system to them, the likelihood of successfully persuading other sections of the public of the validity of a movement's case, etc.

A second major theoretical difficulty is Touraine's conception of social action. Although his methodological writings are characterized by an insistence on the centrality of action, his own conception of it is rather narrow. In particular Touraine shows little interest in what might be called the strategic nature of action, that is the element of means/ends calculation involved in decision-making. In chapter 5 I shall argue that only if action is understood in relation to the actor's assessment of the context and the possible outcomes of alternative courses of action, can processes of mobilization be understood. The importance of Touraine's account of action over the theories I shall later consider is his emphasis on its normative character, but his concern with ideology over organization and pragmatic context leads him to ignore elements of calculation and self-interest.

Finally, the tension between Touraine's social action theory and his periodization of industrial and post-industrial society, with its deterministic and teleological overtones, is not resolved. The theory of social action leads to a general sociological model which plays down the routine nature of most social action and inverts the values of functionalism by replacing stability with instability as the normal condition of social life. On the other hand, Touraine criticizes functionalism for explaining action exclusively with reference to external (social-structural) elements. However, his own theory of post-industrial society is not without deterministic overtones in its claim that there is only one true movement for any given era. To argue in this way is to treat society as a coherent set of social relations in a way that Touraine's own polemic against functionalism would not permit. The argument is then vulnerable to the same criticism as Touraine and Melucci level against functionalism: 'when instances of collective behaviour appear in a social system, the change which is supposed to be the source of this behaviour is always assumed to be of external origin' (Melucci, 1980, p. 213).

VARIATIONS ON THE POST-INDUSTRIAL SOCIETY THESIS:
NEW SOCIAL MOVEMENTS AND THE RESISTANCE
TO 'INNER COLONIALIZATION'

The Tourainean view that some fundamental change has taken place within Western capitalist societies, which places classical Marxist analysis in need of significant revision and which places new social movements at the heart of any sociological explanation of change, has wide currency not only among social movement specialists, but also among theorists from other traditions.

A form of the post-industrial society thesis is present, for example, in empirical and qualitative research such as Inglehart's *The Silent Revolution* (1977). Inglehart's thesis is that the value systems of Western democracies are undergoing a fundamental shift from material to 'post-material' values. This argument, which Inglehart supports with copious empirical evidence, has been highly influential in the interpretation of the rise of the 'new politics' and the decline of social democratic politics in the West. The argument itself is essentially an empirical rendering of Touraine's theoretical analysis.

Similarly, a form of post-industrial society thesis is present in works of sociological history such as Zygmunt Bauman's *Memories of Class* (1982). Like Touraine and Inglehart, Bauman sees the underlying changes within Western societies as rendering older political divisions, particularly that between Left and Right, irrelevant. New agendas have been set, new publics, and new 'victims' created. Under the conditions of late industrialism old political concepts have to be abandoned or recast:

> The Utopia of equality can now show its other face, which it had neither time nor need to display before. The old face was agreeable. The moral injunction 'it is unjust that I have so little' could be used to lubricate the mechanisms of the mass consumption economy. The other face has another injunction written on it: 'it is unjust to have so much'. (Bauman, 1982, p. 182).

But it is above all in the work of Habermas, particularly *Legitimation Crisis* (1976) and *The Theory of Communicative Action* (1987), that a version of the post-industrial thesis as a means of interpreting contemporary society receives its most systematic articulation. As Habermas's analysis both adds new twists to Touraine's (in many ways similar) argument, and further clarifies the assumptions shared by many commentators on these movements, I should like to discuss his arguments in this final section.

Habermas treats new social movements as indicators of potential legitimation crises in late capitalism. The analysis of legitimation crises is grounded in two basic propositions: first, that 'the political system requires an imput of mass loyalty that is as diffuse as possible' (1976, p. 46); and second, that this requirement must be met at a time when capitalism is changing in certain vital respects. These long-term changes include the expansion of the role of state as economic 'steering mechanism', and its simultaneous expansion into the socio-cultural system in the form of welfare schemes, etc. In both cases this development is associated with an extension of purposive rationality in Weber's sense of *Zweckrationalität* into new spheres of social life.

Combined, these two changes are pre-conditions for possible legitimation and motivational crises. The state's steering of the economy undermines the ideological function of the market. The distribution of rewards and scarce resources no longer appears to be the result of the functioning of a nature-like mechanism over which no rational control can be exercised. Habermas shares Marx's view that the central contradiction in capitalism is that between production as a social activity and accumulation as a private one. But now, with the declining role of the market and consequent re-politicizing of class relations, this contradiction focuses on the political rather than the economic system.

With respect to the socio-cultural sub-system, Habermas argues that a privatized life-world, or what he calls 'civil privatism', focusing upon the family and upon consumption combined with an adherence to at least some traditional values is functional for the economic system; it provides appropriate individual motivations and values: deference, achievement ideology (*Leistungsideologie*), etc. However, both traditional world-views and privatism are challenged by increasing state intervention. Even classical or liberal capitalism had an ambivalent effect on traditional values. Adherence to a strict status hierarchy, for example, may be thought functional for unequal societies, but it is nevertheless contradicted by the claim to competition on an equal footing implicit in market relations. But it is in late capitalism that traditional values such as self-reliance (for example, in respect to looking after poor members of one's family), and privatism are most undermined. The intervention of the state into spheres formerly associated with the community or family renders what were previously private concerns and individual fate into public, and thus political, issues.

This analysis of motivation crises in the cultural sphere is based upon a broader claim than has so far been suggested. Habermas identifies what he considers to be a major shift in the nature of morality in late capitalist societies away from a context-specific morality which appeals to authority and tradition, and towards a 'communicative morality' grounded in rationally retrievable arguments and universalizable norms. This development is similarly associated with rationalization in economic and social life, but with respect to motivation and legitimation this tendency runs counter to the functional requirements of the economic and political systems. In other words, there is said to be a built-in tension between the political and economic systems on the one hand, and the socio-cultural system as supplier of motivations on the other. Habermas sees this moral change in, for example, socialization patterns where there has been a shift away from authoritarian and discipline-based practices, and towards more libertarian practices encouraging self-reflection and the demand that norms be backed by rational argument.

At the level of the political system the consequence of these value and moral changes has been the suspension, particularly among the growing ranks of the better educated, of deference towards state action because it 'comes from above', and the growing tendency to demand that policies be rationally presented and justified. And at the level of the economic system such value changes entail a growing disillusionment with the interrelated cultural characteristics of late capitalism: familial-vocational privatism, consumerism and achievement ideology.

These developments are equated not merely with a historical development, the decline of traditional world-views, but also with an evolutionary process said to be implicit in modernity, that is the further development of the project of the Enlightenment, already achieved by science in the sphere of cognition, towards the universalization of our cognitive *and* normative claims.

The analysis is developed in the *Theory of Communicative Action* where Habermas identifies new social movements with the defensive resistance to the processes of 'inner colonialization' of the *Lebenswelt*. In this later analysis new movements continue to resist the extension of technical rationality into all spheres of social life (inner colonialization) while at the same time they continue to demand higher levels of rational justification in the moral and cultural spheres:

The new problems have to do with quality of life, equal rights, individual self-realization, participation, and human rights. In terms of social statistics, the 'old politics' is more strongly supported by employers, workers, and the middle-class tradesman, whereas the new politics finds stronger support in the new middle classes, among the younger generation, and in groups with more formal education. These phenomena tally with my thesis regarding inner colonialization. (Habermas, 1987, p. 392).[6]

While this subsequent argument adds novel twists to the earlier analysis, the structure of the argument has remained constant. New movements are located in the socio-cultural sphere, and the emphasis of their activities is still on motivation, morality, and legitimation. Likewise, they are defined as both progressive and essentially defensive.

Rather than discuss the broader theoretical issues directly, I wish to examine an area in which one may expect to find evidence of the validity of Habermas's arguments as a framework for understanding Western societies, namely, the nature of and demands made by protest movements. Habermas's analysis, I shall argue, offers only a partial account of the role of social movements and indeed some of the demands made by such movements point in the opposite direction to his analysis.

If late capitalist societies were characterized predominantly by the expansion of purposive rationality and communicative ethics, then one would expect social movements to make the following types of demand:

(1) Extension of the right to participate in the decision-making process to previously excluded groups and in new spheres of decision-making. Such demands may include a move towards participatory rather than representative democracy, and the accountability of administrative decision-making processes to democratic processes of 'will formation'.

(2) Growing state intervention in the cultural sphere in order to minimize the arbitrary effects of market relations especially on disadvantaged groups and individuals. This, if radically

extended, may come to include the demand that distribution
of resources be open to public decision-making rather than
based upon market criteria.

In other words, the state is potentially caught between two
broad types of demand which mutually reinforce each other:
the demand for increased state intervention; and the demand
that intervention be open to rational accountability and general
participation. The more the state intervenes, the more it
undermines traditional values and the more it increases public
expectations.

Much of the activity of social movements in the West does
support this view. The civil rights aspects of the black and
women's movements can be seen as an attempt to extend
political rights already implicit in formal democracy to groups
partially excluded from full citizenship. Citizenship can be
understood here in the narrow sense of political and legal
equality, for example, in extension of the franchise, and more
generally as a social demand for an end to discrimination in the
labour market or the family.

This broader sense of social citizenship does not merely
entail lifting formal barriers to equal participation in social
life, but also an increased state intervention in, for example,
the socialization of children, releasing their mothers back on
to the labour market, or for so-called 'positive discrimination'
to compensate for the effects of political or social inequality
specific to particular groups.

Likewise, perhaps the most significant social movement in
the West, the anti-nuclear movement, can be understood in
Habermasian terms of growing communicative morality. This
is so if we view this movement first and foremost as an attempt
to bring decision-making processes which were previously made
according to technical criteria and within administrative ap-
paratuses into the sphere of public debate and participatory
decision-making.

But Habermas's analysis is less satisfactory where social
movement activities and demands are reactions against those
features of late capitalist society which he considers essential
to it and expanding, and where there is a degree of synthesis

of diverse ideological strands into a more comprehensive anti-industrialism.

We can illustrate this weakness with reference to the West German Green movement which is probably the case Habermas himself has in mind. Habermas's analysis does not capture the full implications of the German Green phenomenon. The ideological character of the fundamentalist wing of that movement does not fit Habermas's model of expanding rationality well. The West German Green movement is characterized by a split between a *Realpolitik* model, adopting the tactics of coalition with the SPD and accommodation of ecological to other interests, and a fundamentalism which accords ecological considerations an absolute priority and rejects not merely the model of the growth economy but industrial society as such (see chapter 4). The following features of fundamentalist ideology are particularly problematic for Habermas's account:

(1) A rejection of any notion of progress through economic development. The liberal model of progress, stressing the intimate relationship between a free market, growth and freedom; the social democratic model, stressing the potential for greater equality of opportunity and higher standards of living implied by economic growth; and the Marxist model, stressing the potential for social transformation in the developing means of production, are all considered to have more in common with each other than any one of them does with ecological alternatives. Each presupposes the possibility of infinite growth and they share an evolutionary conception of society based upon economic development.

(2) The idea of class politics, and of the working class specifically, as a source of social transformation, is likewise abandoned: 'It is the industrial system itself which is about to undo us – not the bourgeois class but the system as a whole in which the working class plays the role of housewife. It would therefore be a most inappropriate strategy for survival to appeal to the interests of the working class' (Bahro, 1984).

(3) Correspondingly, the fundamental point of conflict is not between classes, but between the social world and nature.

Thus industrialism, and not merely capitalism, is identified as the source of conflict, and the absolute limits of the system are themselves thought to be asocial, that is they are equated with nature's limited capacity to absorb the effects of manufacture.

(4) A demand is made for a move away from industrial production and towards small-scale self-sufficient community-based production and the corresponding fall in living standards is accepted.

(5) The stress on community is associated with an appeal to tradition as a source of social meaning and morality, that is, rejection of just that rationalism and universalism underlying Habermas's concept of 'communicative morality'. This manifests itself in, among other things, an attempt to reconstruct myths and/or religious experience: 'Nor can we do without that social and psychological experience which, in times of cultural revolution, has always been associated with religious mobilization' (Bahro, 1984, p. 149).

I do not wish to make too much of the significance of the position I have outlined. It is one line of thought within a movement which commands a support within the populations of some Western countries of around 10 per cent of the mostly young and mostly better educated. Nevertheless, it thematizes elements common to a variety of social movements in the West. The place accorded to myth, for example, has echoes in both the women's movement and black movement, and also in the presence of new religious movements in the West. Also, their strongest appeal is among precisely that section of the population which most clearly displays the characteristics Habermas ascribes to culture in late capitalism. Finally, some elements of this critique have at least an elective affinity with influential neo-conservative thought.

In such an ideology one finds elements which Habermas's analysis would lead us to expect, such as questioning of achievements ideology, but equally, the call for return to community and to some aspects of traditional value systems cannot easily be accommodated within a rationalistic framework. The theme of community commonly found in social movement ideology is not one which fits comfortably with a model of expanding rationalism and secularism within late capitalist societies.

Even with respect to the demands upon the Welfare State from within social movements, the picture is more ambiguous than Habermas's view would lead one to expect. Rather than a straightforward claim on the state as supplier of scarce resources, one finds an emphasis on self-reliance and community-based support. This can be seen in the ecological position outlined above, but it can also be seen in other areas of activity, for example, the squatters' movement in West Berlin. Here pressure on the state took the form of a demand that the squatters' right to the houses they occupied be legally recognized, rather than that such housing should simply be subsidized. Indeed squatting was to a degree an alternative to an existence more directly dependent upon the Welfare State with certain of the state's welfare functions adopted, or re-adopted, by the community through networks of self-help (for example, so-called *Instandbesetzung*[7] – restoration of occupied property).

Likewise, a move towards plebiscites need not be evidence of a shift from a formal representative to a participatory model of democracy. Pressures for plebiscites may be no more than an attempt to inhibit a particular form of state activity, as, for example, in the case of the referendum against the nuclear-power policy of the social democratic government in Austria. Such examples may be understood as attempts to limit state power, or achieve particular outcomes, rather than extend popular participation in the Habermasian sense of partaking in a process of collective formation of the general will.

Nor need such cases be taken as evidence of a generalized legitimation crisis, if by legitimation we mean popular recognition of a government's rights to govern plus an acceptance of the general outlines of formal democracy. The desire to stop governments doing certain things does not entail rejection of the political and legal systems in their entirety. These checking operations may indicate the limits of the sphere in which government action is considered legitimate by sections of the population rather than an undermining of legitimacy as such.

These difficulties do not falsify Habermas's theory in any

strict sense. My point is rather that a theory of historical development based upon evolutionary arguments, even where a careful attempt is made to avoid historical determinism and teleology, will produce a one-sided interpretation of current social and political developments.

Such selective readings of the contemporary social and political scene illustrate difficulties with the approach to sociological explanation that Habermas adopts. He works with a systems theory approach in which the features of one sub-system, say culture, are explained with reference to the requirements they fulfil for other sub-systems. Now, while Habermas is fully aware that there is no necessary correspondence between those functional requirements and their actual fulfilment, indeed his interest is precisely in dysfunctions, he nevertheless assumes that the rationality of capital accounting in the economic system will spill over into political and eventually cultural life. But do we need to assume that the economic system will create society in its image in the way Habermas suggests? In the context of West Germany in the 1970s this conception had considerable plausibility. Purposive-rational steering of the economy through neo-corporatist arrangements combined with a developed welfare system characterized peak-level decision-making processes and social arrangements. But in the meantime not only the types of social movement demands I have characterized here, but also conservative parties and governments in the West have challenged this model.

The problem for Habermas is to show that the features he believes essential to late capitalism are in fact essential to it, and are not merely trends associated with particular historical conditions. Were one to rewrite *Legitimation Crisis* now in the context of the early 1990s one could perhaps make out a plausible case that forms of 'authoritarian populism', said, for example, to characterize Britain, were functional requirements for the legitimation of late capitalism. As one major Habermas commentator, Thomas McCarthy, notes:

Even if we grant that normative structures and motivational patterns are undergoing profound change, the question remains as to where these changes will lead. Might they not, for instance, issue in some altered constellation of passivity, privatism, and consumerism no less functional for the formally democratic welfare state? (1978, p. 374).

In adopting a systems theory approach, and especially in combining it with an evolutionary model, Habermas runs the risk of removing certain features of late capitalist society from their historical context and treating them as essential characteristics of the social order, and correspondingly reducing other features to the status of residues of tradition. Non-authoritarian socialization patterns, for example, are treated as indicative of late capitalism, rather than, say, as a middle-class fashion of the 1970s, because they fit both the evolutionary model of expanding *Zweckrationalität* and the systems model view that the logic of the economic system imposes such patterns upon culture.

These types of difficulty stem from the failure of systems theory to demonstrate a correspondence between system needs and adjustments or reactions within what Habermas calls the 'life-world', that is, among social actors. For example, we may succeed in showing a necessary link between purposive rationality in economic life under capitalism and the need to ground norms in a communicative ethic, but this is as likely to develop into a reaction against 'over-rationalistic' and 'over-intellectualistic' moral discussion, and the search for a basis of the normative order in the more secure and less self-doubting sphere of tradition, as it is to produce self-reflection upon our basic normative principles.

The reactions and perceptions of social actors are inde-terminate *vis-à-vis* those systemic characteristics we objectively identify. In divorcing his account of late capitalist society from the practical orientation of the life of the social actor, and the strategic orientation of politics, Habermas imputes a greater degree of purposive rationality to late capitalist society than subsequent developments seem to suggest. Again to quote McCarthy, '[The theory of legitimation crisis] relies to a certain extent on the use of unreconstructed systemic-theoretic conceptions and assumptions; as a result, the practical-political activity of social agents tends to recede into the background'

(1978, p. 379). The sociological consequence of this is an underestimation of the flexibility of late capitalist society to accommodate itself to possible legitimation and motivational crises. We need not assume, as Habermas does, that the choice is between growing rationalism and, in Weber's sense, disenchantment on the one hand, and systems crises on the other. Nor need we assume that the challenge to late capitalism will come from the demand that the cultural consequence of this disenchantment – the call for rational justification of norms – be taken to its logical conclusions.

CONCLUSION

I have discussed Habermas's arguments in some detail because they illustrate an important feature of the post-industrial thesis which is not made so explicit, or even denied, by other advocates, namely, its grounding in evolutionary and system-theoretical explanation. In the following chapter I shall return to the new social movements themselves in order to consider whether the examination of their main ideological strands from such a sociological position offers a plausible interpretation of these movements.

I have suggested that the macro-level theories of new social movements assume a degree of homogeneity in movement form and ideology. In the case of Touraine, it seems clear that he is seeking some social movement which is broad enough to synthesize elements of existing oppositional movements into a coherent ideological and practical challenge to the values and structure of post-industrial society. In other words the funda-mental motivation of much of the theory of social movements within sociology remains essentially Marcusian in inspiration, that is, it is a search for some substitute for the working class, for a new focus of opposition to society in its totality. In this chapter I have raised some general difficulties with this move. In chapter 4 I shall argue that, even in the case of the more spectacularly successful new social movements, there is a degree of ideological and strategic ambiguity, and that it is premature, to say the least, to assume that they are necessarily either progressive or regressive forces.

4
Varieties of ideology within the ecology movement

In treating ecological ideology I wish to consider issues raised by the theories discussed in the previous chapter: Does the ecological critique of growth constitute a new and unique ideology? Does it transcend previous ideological and political divisions, in particular that between Left and Right? I shall argue (i) that while ecological ideology (more accurately ideologies) may provide a new synthesis, its components display vital elements of continuity with traditional anti-capitalist and anti-industrial ideologies; (ii) that ecology (and new social movements in general) also reproduce contradictions between already existing ideological positions. I thus wish to question the claim that 'post-industrial Utopias' transcend older divisions, such as that between Left and Right.

The point of this analysis is not to question the significance of ecology, nor to trivialize the issues to which it draws our attention. My aim is rather to ask whether sociological analysis leads us to expect the wrong things from ecological arguments. Since ecological movements have had their greatest impact in West Germany, this discussion will focus in the first instance on positions within the Green movement there, though I shall also discuss the arguments of the influential French eco-socialist André Gorz.

IDEOLOGICAL STRANDS WITHIN THE
WEST GERMAN GREEN MOVEMENT

West Germany inherited disparate political groupings from the students' movement of the late 1960s. Extra-parliamentary activity was characterized neither by a single dominant force, nor by agreement as to the form such political activities should take.

What Alberto Melucci has called the 'social movement sector' can in the case of West Germany in the 1970s be roughly divided into the following:

(1) *A number of small left-wing parties*: the so-called *Alternativen* and *Bunten Listen* such as the Kommunististischer Bund and the German Communist Party (KPD), as well as anarchist groupings known as 'Spontis' (spontaneists).[1]

(2) *Urban squatters' movements and 'self-help networks'*: The 'Spontis' were closely associated with an urban 'alternative scene' (*die Szene*) whose activities were focused upon lifestyle and the development of community-based self-help networks of which the West Berlin *Netzwerk Selbsthilfe* was the most famous.

The urban character of the *Spontiszene* and of the self-help networks was also reflected in their overlap with squatters' movements in large urban centres such as Frankfurt, Hamburg and West Berlin (see Katz and Mayer, 1985). The squatters' movement in West Germany did not confine itself to house occupation, but also involved renovation of extensive areas of run-down housing – *Instandbesetzung* – to a degree where sections of larger cities were becoming informally renovated through the direct action of their citizens. The squatters' movement was thus able to create a social and physical environment in which alternative lifestyles and politics could flourish.

(3) *'Citizens initiatives' (Bürgerinitiativen)*: The early 1970s saw the proliferation of hundreds of locally-based single-issue initiatives whose initial purpose was to oppose plans which directly affected the local environment, for example, road-building, building of power stations.[2] These citizens' initiatives provided a crucial stimulus to, and basis for, the

later development of the anti-nuclear energy movement and the environmental movement in West Germany.

While most citizens' initiatives remained localized, and of largely local significance, those organized around opposition to the building of nuclear power stations, such as at Wyhl am Kaiserstuhl in 1975, and to the proposed west runway at Frankfurt airport took on a national significance. Because they challenged major projects, and in the case of the nuclear power stations a national nuclear programme, and because of the strength of the opposition and extent of clashes between police and demonstrators, these particular protests politicized the issues around which the citizens' initiatives had become organized.

(4) *Single-issue movements*: From the mid-1970s issue-centred social movements developed out of the citizens' initiatives (see Brand, 1984, chapter 3). In particular the peace movement, partially as a reaction to Chancellor Schmidt's commitment to NATO's double-track policy, the women's movement and the ecology movement became active at this time:

> Within the citizens' initiatives, the ecological movement, the women's movement and in the developing sub-cultural alternative scene began an intensive phase of self-searching, self-reflection, experimentation, project development and mutual accommodation. (Brand, *et al*, 1984, p. 84).

Two further factors provided a significant impetus to the development of an institutionalized ecological movement: first, the consequences of the terrorist acts of the Baader-Meinhof group in the late 1970s, and second, the violence of the clashes between police and demonstrators at the Brockdorf nuclear power station site. The Baader-Meinhof terrorist campaign triggered a strong reaction from the state in late 1977 (the *Deutscher Herbst*) which included a rapid escalation of surveillance and the systematic searching of areas and houses suspected of being centres of subversive activity. In effect, if not in law, extra-parliamentary activity was criminalized.

The movement away from extra-parliamentary activity and towards institutional politics among opposition groups in West Germany was thus, perhaps paradoxically, a reaction to state measures which followed the Baader-Meinhof campaign. Non-violent protest became, and has remained, a central theme of Green politics in the Federal Republic, and civil disobedience combined with traditional political activity – party building, putting up candidates in local elections, etc. – has increasingly replaced direct confrontation.[3]

Anna Hallensleben (1984) identifies three stages of the development of the West German Green Party: (i) the formation of various regional Green groups into local protest parties (mid-1970s to 1979); (ii) the formation of a union of Green groups at federal level (the 'Sonstige Politische Vereinigung' (SPV) Die Grünen), and later the amalgamation of a number of the larger regional parties into a single party (Die Grünen) in order to stand candidates in the 1979 European elections; (iii) after 1979, the entry of Green candidates into various federal parliaments and, after 1983, into the Bundestag.[4]

Each phase posed distinct ideological and organizational dilemmas. The citizens' initiatives from which the German Green Party sprang were characterized by ideological diversity and a wide social base: 'The strength of the Citizens' Initiative movement lay in its wide socially heterogeneous basis, and its organizational form. This was combined with a consciously ambiguous "ideological" armoury' (Mez, 1987, p. 265). There was nothing in the activities of citizens' initiatives which entailed a strong sense of ideological identification. Indeed the ideological diversity of the citizens' initiatives can be counted as one of its strengths, given the breadth of its support among diverse sections of different local communities. This ideological diversity carried over into the early period of the formation of the Green Party. Prior to the formation of the Green Party, as Hallensleben notes: 'The Green Lists were quickly successful precisely because they did not have a political programme, nor did they have to carry any ideological ballast rich in conflict potential' (Hallensleben, 1984, p. 155).

The eclecticism of the Green movement led some commentators to characterize the Greens as neo-conservative rather than leftist, at least in the early stages of their development (see Schäfer, 1983). Evidence in support of this interpretation comes from the significance of a conservative grouping led by ex-CDU politician Herbert Gruhl (Grüne Aktion Zukunft – GAZ) during the initial phases of the party's development. The GAZ opposed the opening of the Green movement to the Left, and rejected the radical organizational principles, such as the rotation of official positions, which were meant to distinguish a Green Party from the established parties.

The crucial change in the political complexion of the West German Green movement came about with the formation of the party, at which point leftist groupings, now committed to parliamentary democracy, joined despite conservative opposition.[5] The crystallizing of Left/Right positions within the movement had already taken place before the launching of Die Grünen in Karlsruhe in 1979 and the agreeing of a party programme in Saarland the same year.[6]

After 1979 the Green Party started to break through the 5 per cent barrier in federal elections.[7] In the 1983 national election Green MPs were elected to the Bundestag. The election of Green candidates at local, federal, and eventually national level sharpened the dispute within the movement between the so-called 'Fundamentalists' ('Fundis') – crudely, those who refuse compromise with established parties or on matters of principle – and 'Realists' ('Realos') – those who are prepared to take part in institutional politics and even form coalitions with existing parties where those parties make concessions on ecological demands. It is to this basic ideological division that I should now like to turn.

Those favouring a fundamentalist position insist that the Green movement remain a movement, and are acutely sensitive to the implications of assuming conventional party or pressure group tactics: incorporation into existing political practices, and a dilution of principles, shifts of the balance of power to the parliamentary section, etc. On the other hand, those committed to *realpolitik* point to the ineffectiveness of such a principled position in bringing about any shift of policy towards ecologically desirable ends.

The continuing debate between realists and fundamentalists within the West German Green movement has concentrated on three issues: (i) principles of organization; (ii) the attitude towards institutionalized politics and specifically the relationship of social movement to political party; (iii) the possibility of a coalition with the SPD. With respect to the first issue, fundamentalists have stressed the danger of oligarchy implicit in organized social movements, and they point to unions and social democratic parties as illustrations of the developments they fear. To combat the tendency towards oligarchy, a system of rotation of leading members was adopted within the movement. There has however been a tendency to move away from strict rotation within the Green Party, with the Realos pointing out the necessary loss of expertise and competence entailed by the removal of experienced activists, and their replacement with less experienced individuals. Even more contentious has been the issue of wages for activists who become elected to positions within federal parliaments, or who become MPs in the Bundestag. Similarly the fundamentalists have not succeeded in their insistence that the financial rewards of becoming an MP in the Bundestag or in the federal parliaments belong to the movement, not to the individual.[8]

In questions of tactics both fundamentalists and realists have accepted the necessity of some engagement in institutionalized politics: standing for elections, sending members to federal and central parliaments, and so on. Nevertheless, there is a basic difference in the way such activities are viewed. Fundamentalists adopt a highly instrumental attitude towards institutional politics in general, and parliamentary politics in particular. The purpose of such activity is to create a public forum in which ecological ideas can be articulated and transmitted through the media at a national level. Parliamentary and institutionalized politics become a means of ideology formation and dissemination. There is no point in expecting institutionalized politics to bring about the desired changes, since such politics necessarily function by conceding enough to groups who have nearly pushed their way into real power to incorporate them, but not so much as to affect real change. A commitment to institutionalized politics alone would merely strengthen the system by legitimizing it further, for example, by persuading those deeply disillusioned with representative democracy once more to vote and participate in the formal democratic processes. For fundamentalists; radical change of the system cannot be achieved within it.

In contrast, for the Realos pragmatic changes can be secured through conventional political means. Incremental improvement can only be brought about through a flexible policy which pressurizes existing institutions, especially political parties, through a mixture of parliamentary activity and, in relation to specific contentious issues, mass mobilization. Realists are not as pessimistic about achieving change through institutionalized means, but nor do they abandon extra-parliamentary activity as an alternative lever of change. Unlike the fundamentalists, for whom institutionalized politics are synonymous with a loss of principles and decay of the movement, realists argue that so long as a fetishism of parliamentary rules and assumptions is avoided, and as long as the parliamentary wing does not gain ascendence over the movement (as happens in the case of social democratic parties), any 'iron law of oligarchy' can be circumvented.

It is however the third issue – possible coalition with the SPD – which has produced the most heated debate between the two sections. I shall use this discussion to illustrate the differences between the two positions. Given the SPD's weak electoral position since the resignation of Helmut Schmidt in 1983, coalition with the new minority party has been on the political agenda for the Social Democrats at both federal and national level. The so-called 'Hessen experiment', in which the SPD governed Hessen in coalition with Die Grünen from 1985 till 1987, provided a model for possible future electoral alliances at national level. More recently the SPD have formed a coalition government with the Alternative Liste in normally CDU dominated West Berlin, after the city's election in January 1989. The coalition is viewed, not least by West Berlin's SPD mayor Walter Momper, as a model for a possible coalition at national level. 'Red-green' coalitions are increasingly seen in West Germany as the most likely alternative to centre-right domination or 'grand coalitions' between the two major parties. With growing support for ecological parties in Western Europe generally, examples such as Hessen and West Berlin may take on a wider significance.[9]

The SPD has itself been divided on the issue, on the one hand aware of its electoral weaknesses, on the other fearing the loss of traditional voters to the CDU/CSU or to the liberal FPD. Significantly, the rejection by the party leadership of any association with the Greens at national level did not prevent exactly these losses occurring in the general election of 1987.[10]

The prospect of being courted by the SPD has produced lively discussion within the Green Party, which again split along Fundi/Realo lines. Joschka Fischer – Green environment minister in Hessen at the time of coalition – and like-minded realists view coalition as an opportunity to exert pressure on the established party which will move the SPD in the direction of ecological politics, or at least squeeze concessions out of it.

This tactic implies a relatively conventional conception of the role of a minority party, and of political parties in general: 'I am convinced that we must not abandon the attempt to build an alternative majority. That means we must adhere to the way of qualitative reform. That means, furthermore, that our operable policies must be clearly formulated' (Fischer, 1985, p. 199). Fischer commits himself to a classical conception of the role of minority parties: coalitions with larger parties as a means of political influence. The inspiration here is the small FPD which through coalition with SPD and CDU/CSU alternately has come to exercise an influence in the political life of West Germany quite disproportionate to its size and electoral support. The conventionally political character of the realists' programme and tactics is made explicit by another leading representative, Otto Schily: 'The political desire of the Greens, and here it is hardly distinguishable from that of existing parties, is to make demands. The government, of course, serves as the preferred target of these demands' (Schily, 1985, p. 275).

This is a conception of politics criticized, not to say ridiculed, by fundamentalists within the movement. Their critique is expressed with great flare and rhetorical skill by Rudolf Bahro, who believes that any such coalition would inevitably draw a politically naïve party into the hands of skilled politicians – people who, while aware of the need for external political support, are also conscious of how to ensure that support through minimum concessions: '[The SPD] drum us into sharing responsibility for the spiral of death which, together with big money and big industry, they carry through' (Bahro, 1985, p. 47). Bahro's dismissal of the SPD is unreserved: 'How can any knowledgeable person today still wish to have a hope for something like the SPD?' (ibid., p. 65). His attitude is based upon a firm belief in imminent ecological catastrophe which makes coalition, or more generally, any form of pragmatic reformist politics, irrelevant. In Bahro's view we are faced with a simple choice: total change or total catastrophe. The ecological movement must aim not at narrow parliamentary politics, but at creating a new populism based upon as wide an appeal as possible: 'In order to save themselves, the Greens – in the wider non-party sense – now need a great flood [of support] from all sections of society: sensitive and cultivated non-conformists, for whom the question revolves around a new totality' (ibid., p. 73).

Bahro's views are shared by other influential members of the West German Green movement such as Petra Kelly:

How can a fully washed-out . . . party like the SPD be a bearer of hope for, of all things, extra-parliamentary peace, conscientious objectors, women's, Third World, and ecological movements, after their record has been so disappointing in these areas? (Kelly, 1985, p. 148).

Underlying Bahro's opposition to coalition with the SPD is a complex societal critique. His arguments, perhaps more than those of any other intellectual of the ecology movement, locate the points of tension between socialist and ecological thinking.

The critique of 'actually existing socialist' societies which Bahro developed at length in *Alternatives in Eastern Europe* (1977) was distinguished from other 'dissident' writings in its adherence to the tradition of Marxist social criticism. His development subsequent to his exile in West Germany has, however, taken him in another direction: towards an eco-fundamentalism the basic tenets of which stand in diametric opposition to Marxism.

The ecological arguments Bahro has developed since the late 1970s articulate the ideological standpoint of the fundamentalist position within, but also beyond, the German Green movement. Its main arguments can be summarized as follows:

(1) All major post-Enlightenment Western ideologies, with the exception of conservatism and romanticism, assume some notion of progress. A faith in progress unites liberals, Marxists, and social democrats. Bahro, like nineteenth-century romantic critics of the Enlightenment such as Adam Müller, rejects the idea of universal human progress. The Enlightenment, the development of capitalism, and the 'rise of the West', are historical accidents not historical inevitabilities.

(2) Bahro is particularly critical of the equation of progress with the economic growth and development implicit in much social theory, from modernization theory to social democracy and within Western political practices. In contrast, borrowing E.P. Thompson's concept of 'exterminism', he views the growth model, and the nature of the West generally, as inherently destructive.

(3) The social structures sustained by continued economic growth do not – *contra* Marx – foreshadow a world-historical development; they are unique and fragile structures which cannot be sustained in the light of ecological pressures: 'The choice . . . is between the more or less peaceful dismantling of the huge structures we have built, and the collapse of the whole system' (Bahro, 1984, p. 147).

(4) Again in contra-distinction to liberalism, social democracy, and Marxism, Bahro dismisses the possibility that the growth model can be exported to the Third World; the eco-system can simply not sustain the demands already placed upon it by the industrialized societies.

(5) The only viable means of averting ecological catastrophe is the importation of small-scale models of production into the industrial societies.

(6) With respect to Marxism, Bahro maintains that the working class cannot be agents of progressive change since they too have a stake in the growth model: 'If I look at the problem

from the point of view of the whole of humanity, not just from that of Europe, then I must say that the metropolitan working class is the worst exploiting class in history' (1984, p. 184).

Bahro is a powerful, articulate and relentless critic of industrial society. His warning is clear, and his solutions are unambiguous. But his arguments, and those of fundamentalists generally, are vulnerable to two types of criticism from the perspective of the realists. First, the fundamentalist position does not face the issue of the feasibility of their proposals for complex industrial societies even if the will to bring about such change could be secured. Fundamentalists do not tackle questions of distribution and planning within an economy of small-scale production. It is not clear, for example, whether we are speaking of individual self-sufficient communities, or some form of division of labour between communities. If the latter, then questions of central co-ordination and distribution become unavoidable. But even if the communities are to be self-sufficient, how are political relations between them to be regulated? Whichever is the case, how are we to dismantle an international division of labour, a complex industrial system and institutionalized science and technology? Second, it fails to explain how that will could be secured, or to identify agents who could bring about such change. Were Bahro's alternative politically realizable it would have to be possible to persuade considerable sections of the population that it was in their interests to bring these changes about. But how is the German working class, or the Western working class in general, to be persuaded that their major goals and achievements – the Welfare State, increasing standards of living, etc. – were premised upon a basic error? Likewise, how are the poorer populations of the Third World to be persuaded that economic development is not a means to elevate poverty, or that if it were, the consequences would be worse than the problems they resolve? Bahro's call for constraints in the West is unlikely to persuade such people that his is not a recipe for Western ethnocentrism.

These criticisms suggest the essentially Utopian nature of the fundamentalist position both in respect of ends and means: 'The utopians were not merely unworldly about the means needed to bring their perfect futures into being, they also envisaged them as a non-political and non-pluralist form of society, without even the potential for antagonistic interests' (Hirst, 1986, p. 98). The Green movement has enlightened people about the side-effects of the industrial system, it has made them acutely aware of dangers to the natural environment, and it has successfully made protection of the environment a central concern and value for large sections of the population. But Bahro is demanding something quite different, namely, that it become the central social and political imperative.

In Bahro's Utopian vision two things have occurred which make realist objections irrelevant: (i) ecological values become non-negotiable absolutes; (ii) pull is replaced by push as the motivating force of reform; that is to say, ecological reform is recommended not primarily because it is in an individual's or a group's perceived interests, but because the alternative is unimaginably destructive.

The issue is not whether Bahro's vision is correct or not; the point is rather that even if it were correct it is unlikely that social actors would react to that state of affairs in the way Bahro desires. To do so would require an enormous trade-off of short-term interests for longer-term ones. Fundamentalist arguments are what Weber refers to as an 'ethic of ultimate ends' (*Gesinnungsethik*) in which all pragmatic considerations are suspended in the face of a single and absolute imperative – in this case salvation from imminent catastrophe.

Furthermore an ethics of absolute ends grounded in an almost millenarian world-view is potentially counter-productive. While it may shock some into action, it is just as liable to alienate others, and to induce either resignation or cynicism, or both.[11]

Bahro is aware of these problems. His call for a 'cultural revolution' is an attempt to overcome the possibility of the alternative reactions I have described by replacing an everyday rationality, based, in part at least, upon calculation of self-interests with a strictly ego-less rationality of ultimate ends. But the problem is precisely that this would be a revolution: a complete inversion of values. As such it remains an abstract moral imperative. It is no coincidence that Bahro should turn at this point in his argument to religious thinkers and doctrines; for it is in religion, and only in religion, that we can ground the kind of 'other-worldly asceticism' that is ultimately Bahro's solution to ecological problems.[12]

THE PERSISTENCE OF LEFT AND RIGHT WITHIN ECOLOGICAL IDEOLOGY

However significant the Fundi/Realo division is for Green politics in West Germany, and however well it illustrates central dilemmas, as a way of characterizing ideological positions within the movement it is too general. The fundamentalist/realist division is, in one form or another, common to many oppositional moments; it is the central tactical dilemma for social movements in their relationship with established politics and social institutions. It is, in other words, a form of the revisionist/revolutionary disjunction. Furthermore, it disguises other axes of political and ideological debate: value differences, differences in ultimate aims, or in the nature of the societal critique.

The notion of an anti-growth, or anti-industrial ideology is likewise too general: romanticism, syndicalism, anarchism, some forms of conservatism, and, in its *Blut und Boden* guise, fascism are all anti-industrial ideologies.

The position of eco-socialism has been influentially expressed by the French ecologist André Gorz, and I shall discuss his views before going on to consider briefly more conservative expressions of ecological ideology.

Eco-socialism

The common denominator between varieties of ecological ideology is the view that traditional socialist politics tied to the working class as agents of social change are no longer applicable, if they ever were. In the case of Gorz this takes the form of a vehement critique of Marxism which, as Giddens points out, appears to have more in common with rightist critics than it does with leftist ones (Giddens, 1987b). Like Bahro, Gorz believes that the working class is no longer a force for progressive change, and that this has profound consequences for oppositional politics.[13] Nevertheless, Gorz still attempts to link an ecological politics to a broadly 'materialistic' analysis of tendencies within the industrial societies, and his conclusions remain in some respects recognizably socialist.

Gorz's arguments represent eco-socialism in that they embody the shift by sections of Left thinking towards eco-socialist positions. This is illustrated in the contrast between his two most influential works *Strategy for Labour* (1967)[14] and *Farewell to the Working Class* (1982). Both works are critiques of consumerism as alienating; both call for a liberation from work; and both call for the creation of a non-capitalist life-style the aims of which are broader than wage increases or improved working conditions. Commenting on these elements of continuity, Gorz writes:

> My critique of the destructive and wasteful capitalist growth model, aimed at maximizing consumption and human dis-enfranchisement, at that time already contained many of the later ecological themes. The socialist lifestyle, as we called it then, which we envisaged, should rest upon the extension of public services and community arrangements, co-operative self-help and self-reliance; and be much less goods and wage intensive. (Gorz, 1986, p. 388).

The major difference between the earlier and more recent positions is the change of the agent whose actions are likely to bring about these changes. Whereas the earlier work develops a theory of factory-based action calling on workers to adopt broader aims than those of traditional trade unionism, Gorz now argues that wage labourers (those who sell their labour for wages) form too narrow a social base to enable us to achieve these goals. In addition, many of those in work behave like 'owners of their jobs', and perceive their interests narrowly as the protection of their position, jobs and living standards against those out of work, or in weaker positions in the labour market. It is to those in the latter category of the un- and under-employed – the 'non-class' of 'neo-proletarians' – that Gorz, like Marcuse before him, now turns in seeking a new emancipatory force.

The course of the eco-socialist position can only be understood against the background of its engagement with orthodox Marxism. In Gorz's case the argument proceeds in several stages from critique to positive Utopian proposal. Gorz first calls into doubt the warrant for the orthodox argument that the working class bears an emancipatory potential of which it is not, or not yet, fully aware. For Gorz, the claim to 'know' the potential consciousness of the proletariat rests upon a mystifying Hegelianism of which orthodox Marxism is guilty. 'Orthodoxy, dogmatism and religiosity are', he writes, 'therefore not accidental features of Marxism. They are inherent in a philosophy structured upon Hegelianism . . . the prophetic element it contains has no other basis than the revelation that came to the prophet himself' (Gorz, 1982, p. 21).

Three changes in particular make it especially problematic to ascribe liberating powers to the proletariat in contemporary capitalism. First, power has become increasingly depersonalized so that it is difficult to identify capitalist 'enemies' as persons, and, likewise, the state becomes less obviously a 'capitalist state'. Gorz makes this point by an implicit appeal to conventional sociological arguments current in the 1960s, for example the 'managerial revolution thesis':

The monopoly capitalist state can no longer be considered – as the traditional bourgeoisie state once was – to be an emanation of the power exercised by the bourgeoisie within civil society . . . Through the sheer size and concentration of its economic units, capital is no longer subject to the influential control of its juridical owners and, having broken the framework of bourgeois law, now requires centralized state regulation and possibly (although not necessarily) state ownership as conditions of its scientific management. (Gorz, 1982, p. 42).

Second, Gorz, who adheres to a strong form of Braverman's de-skilling thesis, denies that the experience of the work-place is liable to induce any form of revolutionary consciousness, especially as technology makes the experience of work increasingly opaque and alienating. The argument here is that only those who have experienced autonomy can have a conception of a non-alienated existence. Like Bauman (1982), Gorz argues that earlier generations of proletarians had experiences, or at least memory, of work not bound by capitalist work discipline, or strict work-times. In contemporary capitalist society it is only outside work that individuals can gain any experience of 'the realm of freedom'.

Third, proletarians, in the strict sense of those who sell their labour for wages, constitute a demographically and socially declining base for a socialist politics. Here Gorz invokes a strong dual economy thesis: the economies of monopoly capitalist societies are increasingly characterized by a workforce divided into a minority of 'core workers' working long hours for high wages; and larger numbers whose experience of work, if it exists at all, takes the form of periodic, insecure and often part-time jobs of limited duration and low reward. This development Gorz also traces back to technological changes: 'This non-class encompasses all those who have been expelled from production by the abolition of work, or whose capacities are under-employed as a result of the industrialization (in this case, the automation and computerization) of intellectual work' (Gorz, 1982, p. 68). The substantive proposals of the eco-socialist position follow from this argument: if the work-place is no longer the focus of radical opposition, the aim of radical politics must be the liberation *from* work and not, as previously, control *over* it.

The types of arguments Gorz articulates are echoed in the eco-socialist strand of the West German Green movement. The notion of a liberation from work has been translated into a demand for a radical shortening of the working week and a breaking down of the division of labour.[15]

The difficulty for eco-socialism is how to differentiate itself from traditional revolutionary socialism on the one hand and eco-fundamentalism on the other. Many of the arguments of eco-socialists sound identical to the more labourist position from which they attempt to distance themselves. They remain distinctive in identifying capitalism, rather than industrialism, as the source of environmental damage:

> The eco-socialists take a more radical position *vis-à-vis* large-scale private property. They emphasize that the destructive tendencies of the production system have their origin in the

frenzy of capital accumulation, which derived not from the individual entrepreneur nor from the politician who defends his or her interests but from the demands of competition. (Hülsberg, 1988, p. 185).

The question which arises here is whether this argument can mobilize greater support in an ecological guise than it did previously. The eco-socialist position, which has been more 'radical' than that of the realists who are committed not merely to institutionalized modes of political action but also to a planning/market mix, has made the Greens vulnerable to Right rhetoric; this brands the would-be 'new politics' with the labels of the old, that is, it identifies them with leftist/communist forces (see Hülsberg, 1988, chapter 10).

On the other hand, in so far as eco-socialists commit themselves to a radical critique of the division of labour, as Gorz does, the distinction between eco-socialism and fundamentalism becomes blurred, and the problem of whether the ends are realizable arises once again. The problem comes out neatly in an interview between Gorz and Peter Glotz, a leading figure in the SPD, when Glotz comments:

> I cannot share your premature egalitarian image of managers spending a week with the refuse collection not least because my own work load would explode. I advocate differentiation of work-time because it would otherwise be extremely difficult to get the public services, chemical or metal branches to pledge themselves to a *single* strategy. (Gorz, 1986, p. 396).

Eco-conservatism

With the possible exception of eco-fundamentalism, ecological positions we have so far considered are of the Left, or at least develop out of a position which is recognizably left-wing. But it is important to recognize that the arguments which sustain the ecology movements are not necessarily Left arguments. Particularly during its early development, several leading figures in the West German Green movement attempted to re-articulate conservative anti-industrialism in ecological terms. The politically most important figure in this development was Herbert Gruhl, who was for ten years a CDU MP and for some of that time its speaker on environmental issues. Gruhl left the CDU to help form the nascent Green Party, but broke off from it to form his own centre-right party (Grüne Aktion Zukunft), after it became clear that the Green Party was taking a leftward turn.

Gorz and Bahro may have reached conclusions which are hostile to Marxism, but conservative critics such as Gruhl see ecology as a means of developing a non-socialist, or anti-socialist, opposition to consumerism and industrialism: 'While Karl Marx understood and attacked the exploitation of people by people, we attack the exploitation of the earth by humanity. But here ends the similarity' (Gruhl, 1984, p. 15). What unites conservative elements within German ecology, apart from their anti-socialism, is the view that the commitment of the CDU and CSU in the postwar period to growth, to the German 'economic miracle', has suppressed strands of earlier (*Altkonservativ* and Romantic) anti-industrialism. Thus another conservative ecologist, Carl Amery, argues that 'the political and social fate' of German conservatism in the postwar period:

> is closely tied to the rise of a new social and economic coalition which in this form had not been seen in Germany. I mean the coalition of heavy industry, the banks and the recently expanded technocracy with the Catholic party machines of Bavaria and the Rheinland. (Amery, 1983, p. 16).

This argument echoes, from the Right, a common ecological theme, namely, the identity of mainstream conservatism with socialism and social democracy, at least on the question of economic growth. Writers such as Gruhl and Amery are essentially arguing for the reconstruction of *Altkonservatismus* in an ecological guise. Although Amery professes scepticism that such a reconstruction is still possible, he nevertheless hopes that 'the new social movements and the ecological start of new thinking and sensibilities are sufficiently internationalized that they will be able to further develop a genuine, that is a growing and changing, tradition' (Amery, 1983, p. 19). Presumably we may also hope that this developing tradition may have some elective affinity with *Altkonservatismus*. Gruhl is not so scrupulous. He traces the origins of pending ecological doom to our creation of an 'artificial' that is, social, and thereby non-natural, world, and to the self-deceiving immodesty of our failure not to recognize the superiority of the natural over the social: 'Man's attempt to take responsibility for the regulation of the world into his own hands has failed because he has created a system outside nature' (Gruhl, 1984, p. 345). Here nature – the 'natural' – has become the absolute antinomy not merely of the technological, but also of the social. Gruhl's ideological appeal is to a conservatism grounded in Christian notions of self-sacrifice and the subordination of human needs to superhuman regulation. Nature substitutes for God in setting the limits of what we may justifiably desire, and salvation can only be obtained through the recognition of our place in the natural order: 'The venture of humanity to desire to regulate will succeed only when we act in full accord with the laws of nature. This is a condition of survival' (Gruhl, 1984, p. 345).

IMPLICATIONS OF THE DIVERSITY OF NEW SOCIAL MOVEMENT IDEOLOGY

Having stressed the ideological diversity of ecological ideology, I should like to discuss some of the broader implications of this, both for our understanding of Green movements, and for social movements generally.

The ambiguities of ecological ideology initially produced considerable confusion among left and liberal intellectuals in West Germany as to the nature of the ideological phenomenon which was gaining political influence: was it progressive in its critique of the dehumanizing effects of industrialization, or deeply conservative in its longing for a simpler, communal, even rural, society? If it was the latter, were we not perhaps seeing the reappearance of the spectre of a new *völkisch*, nostalgic, and perhaps rightist critique of capitalism? There was a tendency among the critics of the Green movement to search for one unambiguous ideological line within the movement. As one commentator notes, 'The ecological turn of rightwing-extremism in the Federal Republic was eagerly seized on by left critics as an opportunity to identify brown spots on [i.e. neo-Fascist tendencies in] the Green movement' (Dudek, 1983, p. 27).

Social democrats, even those who, like Peter Glotz, advocated some kind of accommodation with the Green Party, suspected the Greens of having a backward looking and counter-productive attitude:

> From potential coalition partners we need a clear statement on what we [social democrats] call the 'ecological modernization of industrial society'. The basic insight of this project is that the alternative to the introduction and direction of new technologies is not a soft utopia, but rather the way to becoming a third-rate industrial country stuck in the dirt of obsolete industries. (Glotz, 1983, p. 176).

At the same time, conservative critics of the Greens equated them and their tactics of non-violent resistance with anti-democratic forces and totalitarian ideology.

Rather than view ecological ideology as coherent and unambiguous, as its critics and some of its supporters have tended to do, it may be better to view it as disparate and eclectic in a number of respects. First, it has taken elements from existing ideologies – socialism, Marxism, romanticism, social democracy, etc. – and given them an ecological slant. In doing so it has either employed environmental considerations to give a new underpinning to existing positions, or has adapted, sometimes radically, older ideologies for ecological purposes. Recognizably leftist and rightist positions thus remain. Second, these pre-existing ideological cleavages differentiate varieties of ecological ideology. There is no reason to assume that any one of them is more 'authentic' than any other, nor that these differences will simply disappear as ecology as a political ideology develops.

Recent Marxist discussion of diversity of ideologies within the social movement sector has drawn out some of these broader implications of the proliferation of ideological standpoints for our interpretation of social movements and for the theory of ideology. I shall round off this discussion by considering some of the points to emerge from this debate.

The diversity of new movements in terms of their aims and ideologies has led some Marxists – or 'post-Marxists' – to argue that non-class movements cannot simply be substituted for class, and that a major revision of the assumptions of class theory is required.

The point can be illustrated by contrasting the recent revisionist arguments of Barry Hindess, with the strong Marxist position expressed by G.A. Cohen:

> A person's class is established by nothing but his objective place in the network of ownership relations, however difficult it may be to identify such places neatly. His consciousness, culture, and politics do not enter the definition of his class position. Indeed, these exclusions are required to protect the substantive character of the Marxian thesis that class position strongly conditions consciousness, culture, and politics. (Cohen, 1978, p. 73).

In his restatement and defence of the classical position, Cohen argues that a structural definition of class does not entail a mechanical reading of Marxism, and, more positively, that it is quite legitimate to think of class in these terms. Indeed, to think of class merely as a process, he seems to be saying, is to repudiate Marxism's claim to explanatory power, and consequently to substitute historical or sociological description for theory.

In contrast Hindess, in common with a number of other ex-Althusserians, argues: 'When we examine the forces engaged in particular struggles, we do not find *classes* in the literal sense, lined up against each other. Instead we find political parties and fractions within them' (Hindess, 1987, p. 101). Like-minded commentators on new movements are increasingly making an analogous argument to the effect that diversity along ideological lines, and with respect to broad aims, among social movements makes it unrealistic to expect the development of some unified oppositional force to replace class.

In their more recent writings Paul Hirst (1986), Ernesto Laclau and Chantal Mouffe (1985), and, to a degree, Emanuel Castells (1983), have come to embrace the position which Cohen views as the antithesis of Marxism, namely, a stance which denies that Marxism can be a general theory of society and history, and which goes on to question the possibility of general theory as such. These 'post-Marxists' turn Cohen's question around, asking: If we are not mechanical Marxists, that is, if we no longer accept that consciousness, culture and politics can be read off from structural location, then what explanatory power can a structural definition of class possibly have?

Particularly with respect to discussion of social movements we can detect something of a 'Weberian turn' among Left commentators. Like Weber, they stress the theory's inability to grasp reality in its full complexity, and stress the multiplicity and autonomy of distinct social relations or 'discourses'.

Similarly, they argue that these diverse sets of social relations cannot be reduced to simple antitheses. There are no fundamental social relations from which other relations attain, at most, a 'relative autonomy'. Each societal practice, each discourse, if it is to be understood at all, is to be understood in its own terms. The search for ultimate ends, existing beyond empirically given ends and uniting individual practices into a meta-discourse, is bound to produce theoretical confusion and dogmatic politics.

Such theoretical and political shifts are, I think, in large part traceable not merely to the non-appearance of a unified class actor, but also to the persistent ideological diversity of all oppositional forces.

With respect to social movements the implications of this line of argument have been made most explicit in the work of Laclau and Mouffe. Their recent arguments, like those of Hirst, Jessop and Castells, extend their critique of the Althusserian Marxism to which they earlier adhered. The particular target of their criticism is the claim that certain forms of discourse are 'privileged', that is, have a privileged claim to knowledge because they are 'scientific', or tied to proletarian practices, perhaps. In particular, they deny that such privileged discourses are able to identify the central sets of social relations which hold the key to an understanding of society in its totality. Even the notion of class, and in particular of the working class as a bearer of specific interests, does not enable Marxism to penetrate the appearance of social life and find some rational kernel:

> . . . far from [seeing] a rationalist game in which social agents, perfectly constituted around interests, wage a struggle defined by transparent parameters, we have seen the difficulties of the working class in constituting itself as a historical subject, the dispersion and fragmentation of its positionalities, the emergence of forms of social and political reaggregation . . . which define new objects and new logics of their confirmation. (Laclau and Mouffe, 1985, pp. 104–5).

One critic, Norman Geras (1987), has pointed out, quite correctly, that there are important Althusserian assumptions built into this line of argument. Geras notes that this critique of holistic social theory is an application to structuralist Marxism of its own critical and polemical category of 'expressive totality':

> The concepts in question [expressive totality, etc.] were deployed by Althusser to inscribe a line within Marxism between what he saw as its authentic and its deviant forms. Laclau and Mouffe redraw the line between the whole of Marxism, this erstwhile mentor of theirs included, all vitiated beyond hope of any remedy, and the theoretical outlook they have now come to favour. (Geras, 1987, p. 46).

The outlook which Laclau and Mouffe 'have now come to favour' is discourse theory, though it does not appear to be a theory at all, but rather a tool for posing questions and criticizing the presumptions of theory in general. It is a kind of anti-theory theory. Laclau and Mouffe use discourse analysis to point up the limits of theorizing as an intellectual activity.

Adopting the language of discourse theory renders Laclau's and Mouffe's arguments highly abstract and elliptical. I think, however, they can be reduced to a number of straightforward and quite relevant points.

The first, and most central, implication of the critique of general theory within Marxism for the understanding of social movements is that there is a plurality of struggles: there is a variety of social conflicts, none of which are 'more real' than others; the groups involved in individual struggles do not necessarily share common interests and aims; and if we are to develop a more satisfactory politics, we must recognize this. Furthermore, individual struggles are not necessarily orientated to the same sets of social relations (that is, have a common opponent). Thus, they claim that '*there are not*, for example, necessarily links between anti-sexism and anti-capitalism' (Laclau and Mouffe, 1985, p. 178).

Second, the outcome of these diverse struggles is not predetermined by structural factors, but is the result of developments internal to the movements concerned, and of their reaction with their environment:

> The forms of articulation of an antagonism, therefore, far from being pre-determined, are the result of a hegemonic struggle. This affirmation has important consequences, as it implies that these new struggles do not necessarily have a progressive character, and that it is therefore an error to think, as many do, that they spontaneously take their place in the context of left-wing politics. (Laclau and Mouffe, 1985, pp. 168–9).

The point being made here is banal but has nevertheless been underrated within theories of social movements: the debates which go on inside social movements will in part determine the ultimate character of those movements. Outcomes are not predetermined by interests or structural location.[16] Rather, the form of movement activity and ideology is a reflection of the tendency which becomes hegemonic within the movement. 'Hegemony' thus replaces the idea of structural determination in the argument.

What follows from these two arguments is quite clear: in contrast to orthodox Left theory, and to the views of many new social movement activists, Laclau and Mouffe question the possibility of a united and coherent socialist politics based either on class or new social movements. This final step marks the break between post-Marxism and the revisionist arguments of Marcuse and others.

But is there no potentially unifying political 'imaginary' whatsoever? It is Laclau's and Mouffe's answer to this question which has most irritated their critics (see Wood, 1986 and Geras, 1987). Essentially, Laclau and Mouffe replace socialism with the vaguer notion of 'radical democracy'. This substitution is a direct consequence of the above arguments: socialism is an essentially teleological concept; it forecloses the future by specifying definite and finite ends of specific social practices. In contrast, the notion of radical democracy, like Habermas's 'ideal speech situation', is purely formal: it says nothing about the positive outcomes of historical struggle. For Laclau and Mouffe, this 'vagueness' is precisely the attraction.

Similar arguments are advanced by Paul Hirst in *Law, Socialism and Democracy* (1986). He too is concerned to reject holistic theories of society, and to draw the political consequences of this move. So, for example, of the state Hirst says 'however much it may be presented as a single public power, the "state" is itself a complex of differentiated agencies of decision: ministries, local councils, specialist bodies, etc.' (1986, p. 23). This statement, more than the arguments of Laclau and Mouffe, makes explicit the most radical consequence of these arguments, namely, *it is no longer possible to maintain a distinction between pluralist and institutionalist analysis on the one hand, and some more comprehensive – 'totalizing' – scheme on the other*. There is, in other words, no a priori distinction to be drawn between Marxist and 'bourgeois' analysis.

These broader arguments draw out some of the wider implications of the kinds of ideological diversity I have identified in the West German Green movement. These may be summarized as follows:

(1) There is both within and between new social movements a high degree of diversity of aims and ideology.
(2) This diversity undermines attempts to treat them as coherent and cohesive responses to a single social development, however broad.
(3) It is likewise unrealistic to measure actual movements against some putative meta-political discourse of an ideal movement as Touraine tends to do.

(4) There is no single predictable outcome to the debates and developments that go on within movements which can be deduced from 'objective' interests.

(5) Consequently, social movements are neither necessarily progressive or regressive.

(6) There are important elements of continuity between new social movement ideology and 'traditional' ideological divisions such as those between Left and Right, or reform and revolution.

My argument here departs from that of Laclau and Mouffe on the question of the extreme relativism of their position. This relativism can be seen most clearly in their notion of 'radical democracy' as the – almost transcendental – aim of all oppositional movements. The notion is over-generalized. Any social movement activity can be defined in terms of radical democracy by dint of the simple fact that it aims at loosening the hold of institutionalized 'discourses', be its more concrete purpose the achieving of greater equality or the installation of authoritarian populism.

This relativism stems from the language of discourse analysis in which the argument is couched. First, by using discourse analysis as the medium through which to criticize general theories of social movements, Laclau and Mouffe detach social actors from any institutional constraints, and more generally from any specific social context. Such a position is more pluralist then pluralism in its reduction of politics to discourse. Second, 'discourses' are treated as being essentially incommensurable. Each constitutes a discrete 'form of life' and is thus to be understood *exclusively* in its own terms. But, as we have seen, ecological debates demonstrate the degree of cross-fertilization which exists between competing ideological 'discourses'. The notion of discourses not only excludes the rootedness of ideologies in practical and political concerns, it also vastly undervalues the degree of eclecticism within ideology. There is nothing in ecology to suggest that it is hermetically cut off from competing ideological positions.

Rather than treat ideological diversity as evidence of incommensurability, it may be better to view ecology as ideologically contestable. Ecological issues are in many respects politically and ideologically unoccupied territory; and thus the object of attention from diverse ideological standpoints. Viewed as such, there is nothing necessarily Left or Right about ecology, but as it has developed into a political force the struggles around it have funnelled ecology into pre-existing ideological categories. The diversity of positions within the West German Green movement demonstrates not so much a transcendence of older ideological divisions as the still open-ended nature of the contest around new issues.

Rather than draw strongly relativist implications from ideological diversity among social movements, I shall argue in subsequent chapters that sociological analysis must thematize the institutional constraints and contexts within which mobilization and social movement activity take place. This is consistent with the implication of Hirst's argument that there is no categorical distinction to be drawn between sociological (or Marxist) approaches and pluralist/institutionalist models. It contrasts sharply, however, with the anti-institutional assumptions that discourse analysis shares with the more traditional theories of social movements discussed in chapter 3.

In the following two chapters I wish to re-assert the centrality of institutional analysis through a discussion of micro- and then middle-range approaches to mobilization and political processes.

5

Movements and parties: problems of organization and mobilization

One may speak separately of economics and politics, and speak of 'political passion' as of an immediate impulse to action which is born on the 'permanent and organic' terrain of economic life but which transcends it, bringing into play emotions and aspirations in whose incandescent atmosphere even calculations involving the individual human life itself obey different laws from those of individual profit, etc.

Antonio Gramsci *Prison Notebooks*, p. 140

I have argued that macro-theories of social change have idealized social movements, paying insufficient attention to the problems of organization and mobilization which face any form·of sustained collective action, and underestimating the degree of diversity between new social movements.

An adequate theory of social movements would have to recognize the problematic and effortful nature of mobilization and the consequent organizational constraints. This task has been tackled by theories of 'resource mobilization'. In this chapter I wish to discuss these social action approaches and ask whether general theories can be supplemented by lower-level analysis of organization and mobilization. The mutual indifference that has existed between macro accounts and micro-level theories of resource mobilization has meant that this possibility has largely been ignored.[1]

Resource mobilization theory (RMT) addresses a different order of questions from the approaches so far discussed and appears indifferent to attempts to explain social movement activity with reference to broad social transformations. At the same time RMT has developed a sophisticated analysis of the mechanics of collective action, of the barriers to it, and of the conditions under which it can operate. These models have been applied to a wide variety of social movements providing empirical information on the form particular movements have taken and on how they have overcome, or failed to overcome, problems inherent in collective action.

RESOURCE MOBILIZATION THEORY

The development of RMT as a paradigm within social movement theory was stimulated by the publication of Mancur Olson's seminal *The Logic of Collective Action* in 1965. Taking the argument of Olson and Oberschall as examples, I shall be particularly concerned with the theoretical underpinning of RMT, since it is here that the approach's strengths and weaknesses become most apparent.[2]

The premises of Olson's work are those of neo-classical economics: (i) social phenomena are to be explained with reference to the preferences and choices of individuals; (ii) individuals act rationally to maximize their interests and minimize their costs. Olson's model was both methodologically individualist and grounded in 'rational choice theory'.[3] In the course of its application to social movements, resource mobilization theorists have modified the assumptions Olson carries over from economics in a number of ways. First, subsequent analysis has supplemented these propositions with further assumptions taken from realist political analysis[4] (Oberschall, 1973); second, the strictly egocentric assumptions of economic analysis have been modified in the attempt to take solidary action into account (for example Fireman and Gamson, 1979, and Opp, 1986).

It will be argued that while RMT does help us understand the organizational dilemmas facing social movements, it is handicapped by its continued adherence to economic models of human agency, and says little about the content and context of social movement activity. A sociologically adequate theory of mobilization would have to identify the sources of solidarity which are preconditions for collective action by accommodating expressive, habitual, and affective as well as instrumental orientations for action. This is only possible if we recognize the significance of the cultural, as well as purposeful, aspects of social movement activity.

From Olson on, micro-theories have addressed two related questions: first, given the inherently problematic nature of collective action, how is it possible that agents come to act collectively at all? second, how do organizations, such as trade unions, which depend upon mobilization, overcome, or attempt to compensate for, the deficiencies of collective action?

For RMT, collective action is thought particularly problematic and unstable not because it involves costs for the agent – individual action also involves costs – but because the benefits are non-divisible, that is, they are collective goods. In the case of collective goods, there is no direct correspondence for the individual between the costs involved in acting as part of a collectivity, and the reward one might expect:

> Just as it was not rational for a particular producer to restrict his output in order that there might be a higher price for the product of his industry, so it would not be rational for him to sacrifice his time and money to support a lobbying organization to obtain government assistance for the industry. (Olson, 1965, p. 11).

Because the individual group member receives the collective goods attained by his/her group irrespective of whether or not he/she acts to acquire that good, it is rational to 'free-ride' – that is, to accept the rewards of group membership without making the sacrifices necessary to obtain those rewards. In this way I can receive the collective good without any of the concomitant costs. Where all actors are in an identical position *vis-à-vis* costs and rewards of collective action, a 'prisoner's dilemma' arises in which action is taken and no collective good secured.

This is thought to be a particularly acute problem for large organizations such as parties and unions where sources of interpersonal sanction against free-riding are limited. In such cases, Olson argues, individuals will only be induced to act in the collective interest where the group (or organization) can distribute 'selective incentives', that is, rewards received according to members' contributions: 'The incentive must be "selective" so that those who do not join the organization working for the group's interest, or in other ways contribute to the attainment of the group's interest, can be treated differently from those who do' (Olson, 1965, p. 51). Where the organization can so act the individual will be willing to pay the costs involved in collective action on the expectation that he/she will receive private as well as collective benefits.

In order to mobilize its resources (the energies of its members in collective action) the organization must be in a position to distribute selective rewards. To appeal to the 'collective interest' or group ideals is insufficient (or even unnecessary) since such appeals will not affect my decision to act in accordance with the collective interest.

Olson's theory, and its subsequent modified versions, have predictive powers with respect to collective bodies such as unions, lobbies, parties, and movements, because overcoming free-rider problems imposes specific organizational and tactical imperatives and limitations on these organizations. Resource mobilization theorists have identified the following types of imperative placed upon organizations and movements by the limitations of collective action: (i) the necessity of providing divisible private benefits as well as indivisible collective ones places high organizational costs upon collective bodies; (ii) the search for resources such as external funding therefore becomes a major organizational preoccupation; (iii) at the same time the organization is restricted in the demands and sacrifices it can realistically expect of its members; (iv) thus occasional low cost/low risk tactics ought to be preferable to frequent high cost/high risk activities.

In drawing attention to these factors theories of resource mobilization have been sensitive to the inherent constraints of collective action, a factor which macro-theories largely disregard. RMT implies that the room for manoeuvre for social movements is constricted by the organizational imperative and problems associated with free-riding, and not merely by the external constraints of powerlessness, etc., emphasized in the works of earlier commentators such as Piven and Colward (1977). Collective action is thus viewed as unstable, problematic and occasional.

Because the internal organizational constraints of collective action are thought to pull social movements towards institutionalized forms of activity where the costs/risks are lower and the possibility of gaining external support greater, theories of resource mobilization are drawn towards a realist political analysis of movements, rather than the idealized view which I have argued is implied in macro-level sociological discussions. The attitude towards this institutional pull also distinguishes RMT from more macro-theories. Whereas for Touraine institutional pull is evidence of the immaturity of the movements, for resource mobilization theorists it applies to any form of collective action. Non-institutional collective action will tend to metamorphose into institutional action where the risks, for example of illegality, are lower. Furthermore, loose organization demanding high degrees of commitment from members will give way to tighter more formal organization where the organizational burdens will be taken over by 'professionals' or quasi-professionals, and where demands on grass-roots members will be restricted to occasional meetings, participation in collective action, etc.

RMT, like forms of political realism, stresses both the limits of political action, and the largely instrumental and self-interested nature of that action. We can see affinity between RMT and the realism of American political science more clearly in a second influential contribution to micro-level theories of mobilization: Anthony Oberschall's *Social Conflict and Social Movement* (1973).

While Olson's arguments strictly limit the possibility of collective action and successful mobilization, Oberschall is more sanguine about the possibility of mobilization. There are two reasons for this: first, he argues that social movements are more likely to obtain outside assistance, and hence are better placed to distribute selective incentives, than Olson assumes; second, he widens the notion of incentive, or at least the context of its distribution, to include such social benefits as status, power and class mobility.[5]

This enables Oberschall to identify the social conditions under which mobilization is likely to occur on the basis of a risk/reward model. Opposition movements are liable to arise under conditions where social mobility is restricted, and where access to powerful positions is closed off. Under such conditions, although the risks of sanction remain, the potential rewards of this course of action are, at least for the leaders, greater. For Oberschall the leaders of social movements are 'political entrepreneurs just as politicians are' (1973, p. 159), and as such are likely to adopt social movements as their preferred medium when conventional means (for example, parties) are not easily available to them: 'If the activists pursue selfish goals, they have a stake in continued agitation and provocation that might result in incidents around which the rank and file can remobilize' (Oberschall, 1973, p. 175).

In this way the leaders' interests can coincide with those of their followers, and they can only follow their own interests within the rules of social movements when they articulate group grievance. The situation for group members who do not aspire to leadership is somewhat different. They do not have such high potential gains, but on the other hand their risks are lower. In either case, 'since most people do derive tangible benefits from group membership, they will weigh very carefully the advantages of pursuing private ends in conflict with group goals with the disadvantages of loosing group membership and being exposed to group sanctions' (Oberschall, 1973, p. 75).

Oberschall's arguments are more sociologically sophisticated than Olson's strict economic decision theory, and partially overcome one of the major difficulties of the Olson model, namely, that it seems to suggest the near impossibility of successful collective action. In Oberschall's argument the definition of benefit is broadened and some attempt is made to understand the relationship of movements to their political environment.

We are now in a position to assess the contribution of theories of resource mobilization to social movement theory. Micro-theories of resource mobilization possess advantages over both functionalist sociological models, and general theories of social transformation of the Touraine-Habermas variety.

Unlike functionalism, collective action is treated as rational and is not reduced to an expression of frustration or an irrational outburst. The actor is credited with the capacity for rational calculation, and collective action is itself bound by the rules and limitations of rational action. With respect to theories of long-term change, RMT does not idealize collective action nor detach it from organizational and tactical constraints. Indeed, as we have seen with Oberschall, this approach is closely attached to a realistic analysis of the process of political negotiation, and views the integration of social movements into established or 'institutionalized' politics as a natural progression rather than, in the Touraine fashion, a regression into lower forms of social struggle. In stressing the continuity, rather than discontinuity, between social movements, parties and institutionalized forms of political action such as pressure groups and parties, RMT has developed a more plausible account of social movement development. That is to say, it is one which corresponds more closely to the typical development of social movements rather than counter-factually trying to explain the 'failure' of movements to retain their movement character.

In recognizing the internal constraints of collective action, RMT draws attention to the dilemmas facing social actors at the point at which they choose whether to involve themselves in collective action. Rather than assume that an adequately articulated critique of existing social relations will suffice to secure mobilization, the hidden assumption of macro-sociological discussion theories grounded in methodological individualism stress the element of calculation involved in choosing between the uncertain long-term benefits of social change against the costs of such action, and against the short-term benefits of adhering to the status quo. As the political scientist Adam Przeworski argues in the case of the working class, an undistorted recognition of the exploitative nature of capitalism will not necessarily lead to revolutionary action on the part of workers (1985).[6] Methodologically individualist arguments suggest that there has been an overemphasis on the role of ideology in explaining resistance to collective modes of action.

Furthermore, micro-theories grounded in methodological individualism recognize what these dilemmas of mobilization
mean for the organizational questions facing social movements.
In particular they emphasize the need to overcome the limitations of collective action by building formal organizations, or to
attempt to increase available resources by adopting lower-risk
institutional forms of action. Particularly in Oberschall's case,
as a consequence of the last consideration, the state/actor
relation is re-introduced as a central theme of social movement
activity. In contrast to macro-theories, which typically define
social movements in non-institutional and largely culturalist
terms, resource mobilization theories recognize the complexity
of the relationship between non-institutional and institutional
strategies, and the significance of the politics and state institutions in the developments of social movement activity. Finally,
the model is 'realistic' both in its recognition of the limitations
of collective action, and its assessment of pragmatic political
considerations. It does not ignore the internal and external
constraints acting upon social movements, and there is not the
idealistic assumption that clarity about movement aims and the
correct identification of stakes and actors is a sufficient condition
for successful collective action.

Oberschall's analysis, for example, reproduces two typical
features of American political science: first, hard-nosed political
realism, and second, a concern with political integration and
stability. The view that social movement leaders strive above all
else to integrate themselves into existing political arrangements,
and thereby secure a degree of social and political mobility is
an effective counter-balance to the excessive naïvety of much
of the European discussion of new social movements. As I
shall argue in chapter 6, an adequate sociological model must
acknowledge the constraints acting upon social movements and
theory.

We can illustrate these strengths of RMT by referring back
to the example of the West German Greens. There are several
aspects of the development of the German Green movement
upon which theories of resource mobilization can throw light.
For example, high levels of collective action entail high costs
and risks for those involved and will tend to be short-lived and

focus on specific contentious issues, for example, individual power station sites, building projects. The long-term difficulties in activating support have created a strong pull towards building a formal organization which can carry the movement over the low points of cycles of collective activity. Similarly, party-type and pressure-group-type organization have become attractive options for European Green movements because they demand a lower level of commitment from the rank and file support, and hence entail lower costs. At the same time, there are tangible resources available to these type of organizations which are not available to pure social movements. One obvious example in the German case is the subsidy made available to political parties once they have gained political representation. Thus after 1983 the German Green Party was able to claim campaign expenses. Similar incentives were available to the Green movement in Austria once it too entered parliament in 1987.

These pull factors in the German case were reinforced by a push factor, namely, the state's reaction to terrorism. This made extra-parliamentary forms of activity much more risky than more traditional models of political participation. Furthermore, the central role given to the political entrepreneur by Oberschall has been confirmed by the experience of ecology parties in Western Europe. Despite its grass-roots democratic principles the European ecology movement has indeed thrown up, and often centred around, political celebrities such as Petra Kelly, Otto Schily and Joschka Fischer in West Germany, or Freda Meissner-Blau and Günther Nenning in Austria.

LIMITATIONS OF
RESOURCE MOBILIZATION THEORY

While RMT manages to theorize aspects of social movement activity about which macro-theories remain largely silent, there remain a number of questions about its methodological assumptions. Among these are: (i) Does RMT have a sufficiently broad account of the motivation of social actors to explain their, however occasional, involvement in collective action? (ii) Do social actors, and should we, view social movements in exclusively instrumental terms?

I first wish to discuss the view of social action which underpins theories of resource mobilization. RMT has a narrow, or more critically, impoverished, interpretation of human motivation which reduces it to instrumental rationality. If we take Weber's typification of forms of action (traditional, affective, value oriented and ends oriented) only the last of these – *Zweckrationalität* – is accommodated within the model. I shall argue that the specific difficulties discussed below which are faced by theories grounded in methodological individualism stem from their narrowly instrumental conceptualization of human action.

One such empirical problem for RMT is that, given the free-rider problem, collective action ought to be a more exceptional and rare occurrence than it actually is. Stressing the barriers to collective action is justifiable. Most people most of the time do not act collectively, do not subordinate their own and their family's interests to political ideals, and remain within a private and domestic sphere. But, equally, people occasionally break out of 'civil privatism', and show a remarkable disregard for their self-interest if we define this, as resource mobilization theorists typically do, in terms of personal welfare. Likewise in certain forms of collective action rational considerations in the limited sense of means/ends calculation appear suspended and people risk their lives, freedom and property for an outcome which is neither certain, nor always clearly defined. Prima facie, there is something paradoxical about a theory which suggests the improbability of events which are regular, even if not everyday, features of political life.

Some narrowly instrumental model of action may be accepted as a pre-condition in economic analysis because such simplifying assumptions are pre-conditions for model building; but if they are to be translated into sociological accounts of action they must be descriptively accurate. If we want a sociological account of social movement activity we must treat the assumptions of rational choice theory as empirical rather than a priori presuppositions, and it is as such that I shall now discuss the RMT view of actor motivation.

Oberschall's account of the motivation of leaders and rank and file, for example, is still largely based upon strict notions of self-interest. Risks and rewards are not defined with reference to value orientations, but by reference to universal, though somewhat vague, standards of personal welfare: 'No one is in a position to disregard where his next meal is coming from and whether he is going to have a roof over his head'(1973, p. 159).

The restricted conception of actors' interests leads Oberschall to assume a highly integrative sociological model similar to Smelser's. Whereas for Smelser the chief aim of collective action is to re-establish social equilibrium and hence minimize stress, Oberschall's activist-entrepreneurs are first and foremost concerned to integrate themselves into existing power and status structures and employ social movements as means of social mobility in the absence of more legitimate means. Both presuppose a single legitimate order which is to be maintained or into which individuals attempt to climb.

In many respects strictly *zweckrational* models of action are peculiarly inappropriate for understanding social movements. Such a model asserts that collective mobilization is unlikely except where an organization is established enough and in control of enough resources to distribute rewards selectively to its members in return for co-operation in pursuit of common goals; this seems particularly unfit to explain cases of protest and emerging movements. It is possible to see how relatively rich and established organizations can command mobilization on the part of their members, but it is not clear how such an organization could have become established in the first place, nor how organizationally weaker groups can mobilize at all. This is especially so in cases of social movements which challenge the established order and which are normally in a weak position to distribute selective incentives, all the more since such groups typically act under conditions of considerable uncertainty and even danger and where, consequently, the collective rewards remain obscure and the risks unpredictable and perhaps considerable.

Does the problem of fitting collective action into rational choice models suggest or stem from some deeper methodological or conceptual problem with the model itself? In criticizing rational choice models it is not necessary to appeal to altruism alone or to deny the role of rational calculation and considerations of self-interest and self-protection from risk. Rather we can identify two aspects of RMT which make it vulnerable to general sociological criticism: first, its decontextual understanding of preferences, choices and actions; second, the rigidity of the means/ends distinction it employs.[7]

'Commitment', 'loyalty', 'engagement', etc. – all those concepts which convey an identification with others or with aims which are not strictly instrumental – are excluded from any model of action which grounds social action in instrumental rationality alone. I do not wish to assert the contrary, that social actors are blind idealists, but ∴ is difficult to see how solidary action, or perhaps social life in general, would be possible if the basic hypotheses of a strict rational choice theory were an empirically adequate description of human action and motivation.

Furthermore, while we can redefine terms such as 'loyalty', 'commitment', etc. in such a way as to fit an instrumental model, it is at the cost of loosing their linguistic and social force. As Amartya Sen has observed, 'It is possible to define a person's interests in such a way that no matter what he does he can be seen to be furthering his interests in every isolated act of choice' (Sen, 1982, p. 88). Thus, 'no matter whether you are a single-minded egotist or a raving altruist or a class conscious militant, you will appear to be maximizing your own utility in this enchanted world of definitions' (Sen, 1982, p. 89).

But the price in an impoverishment of language is a high one to pay for the creation of working models. One potential danger is that of teleology: irrespective of the content of my values and perceptions, my actions can always be redefined in terms of self-interest even where my interests appear altruistic or motivated by blind idealism: 'To follow this teleological route is to remove the cutting edge from the selective incentive argument' (Fireman and Gamson, 1979, p. 20).

More specifically, the decontextual character of methodologically individualistic approaches to collective action makes it difficult to address two important and related questions: (i) What is for an agent a cost, and what a benefit?; (ii) How are agents' preferences formed?

One of rational choice theory's most perceptive critics, Albert Hirschman, points out a basic flaw in the language of instrumental models by arguing that attempts to attain collective goods cannot be viewed one-dimensionally as a 'cost' because in such cases the cost/reward dichotomy itself becomes blurred: action can be, to use an apt phrase, 'its own reward'. In other words, our motivations towards collective action are richer and more diverse than instrumental models suggest. Involvement in collective action can, for example, be an expression of an actor's values. I may involve myself in peace activities because that involvement itself demonstrates my commitments, and is consistent with my self-image. In such cases my concern is not exclusively, or even primarily, with the likely outcome of such actions, or the contribution of my participation to their success. In many cases engaged actors participate in collective action knowing full well that the chances of 'success' are limited. In cases of expressive actions where the action is primarily a demonstration of values, means/ends calculations are irrelevant because it is in the action itself that the 'end' is expressed.

This type of criticism is significant because it calls into question two deep assumptions of methodologically individualistic approaches to collective action. In the first place it questions the universal validity of the strict means/ends distinction implied in the notion that action involves a careful weighing up of cost and benefits. If an action can in any sense be its own reward we must recognize at least that actions have an expressive, as well as an instrumental, function for the actor. The normative nature of action, and the notion of action as an expression of values, self-understanding, etc. slips through the net of rational choice explanations.

These criticisms are not merely methodological. They have concrete consequences for our understanding of social movements. Thus, for example, while Olson-type models claim to *explain* collective action, they actually make its occurrence a mystery. Why should an individual actor ever allow him/herself to become embroiled in collective actions when this can never increase his/her overall well-being? The notion of 'selective incentives' does not bridge the gap. If we do not widen the micro-level model of action, it is not possible to account for cases of collective action, especially where outcomes are unclear, organizations weak, etc.

In the second place, more fundamental than the ambiguity of the concept of reward and cost is the question of the formation of agents' preferences. The treatment of agents' preferences and identities as exogenous and given excludes, a priori, vital social processes from analysis. Within the model, the individual is treated as an essentially asocial being whose identity is given, and who is bound to others only instrumentally: 'A general criticism that can be levelled against the Olson analysis – and against much economic decision theory in general – is that its subjects, while efficient and often even ingenious and devious, are *without a history*' (Hirschman, 1985, p. 79). In the following discussion I shall argue that understanding processes in which preferences are formed is central to a sociologically adequate account of social movements, and furthermore this can only be achieved if we recognize the significance of movements as cultural as well as political phenomena. This in turn requires that we locate processes of preference formation within collective action and not merely as an exogenous variable.

In a sense theories of rational choice start from the wrong point: we do not need to compress all possible actions into the narrow funnel of instrumental rationality, but rather we need to find a conception of rationality broad enough to accommodate the variety of action. A micro-level theory of action which underpins an understanding of collective action needs to accommodate both *Zweckrationalität* (action involving means/ends calculations) and *Wertrationalität* (action oriented towards absolute values). To do this we need to address two related question which lie outside the scope of rational choice models: (i) How do agents come to have the preferences upon which they choose and act? (ii) What is the rational basis of solidarity and actions based upon commitment rather than calculation?

Implied in the first question is the possibility that preferences are altered, or formed, in the course of collective action. If this were the case, RMT would have to be radically revised. The constraints to collective action (for example, preferences, and risk/benefit calculations) would not be simply givens to which social movements must adapt themselves if they are to secure support and mobilization, but rather the movements themselves could mould, or at least modify, the agent's perception of his/her interests and preferences, and, at least to a degree, in this way alter the constraints. Rather than treat preferences as an external variable given before choices are made and action taken, we may try to take the formation of preferences as an object of investigation in itself.

Such considerations have led some critics of RMT and rational choice theory generally to suggest that understanding social movements requires an analysis of the processes by which preferences and identities are moulded in discursive processes and in the course of collective action. Claus Offe and Helmut Wiesenthal thus argue that among the chief tasks of social movements is the discursive formation of preferences and identities which transform the consciousness of isolated social actors into a collective or general will:

> [Those] in the inferior power position can increase their potential for change only by overcoming the comparatively higher costs of collective action by *changing the standards according to which these costs are subjectively estimated* within their own collectivity.' (Offe and Wiesenthal, 1985, p. 183).[8]

Offe's and Wiesenthal's intention in 'Two logics of collective action' was to show that structurally the working class, or more generally all subordinate groups, can act in their own interest only through collective action, while capitalists can pursue their class interests while acting in their own immediate interests as individual capitalists. This argument is dubious because, as Marx repeatedly emphasizes, the structural position of capitalists, as in market competition, makes it no less problematic for them to pursue their class, as opposed to individual, interests. As Olson recognizes, free-rider and collective benefit problems may be just as likely to arise among capitalists as among workers. But even if we do not accept this aspect of the argument, the point about the discursive formation of preferences is still important.

Offe's and Wiesenthal's argument draws attention to the central role of social movements in creating an alternative collective will through consciousness-raising, creation of alternative life-styles, etc. This suggests that the culture and life-style of social movements have an important function in processes of mobilization which are ignored in models that view social movements exclusively instrumentally, that is, as organizations with specific aims and interests.

Alberto Melucci's concept of 'social movement sectors' – the loose affiliations and networks from which movements spring – develops the cultural argument further. Melucci's emphasis on the social movement sector is suggestive in that it questions the assumption of RMT that the orientations of actors towards movements are primarily instrumental. By seeking out social spheres which cultivate alternative life-styles, etc., the social actor is also looking for an alternative social identity:

> [What] women, along with other contemporary collective actors, have achieved is above all to practise alternative definitions of sense: in other words, they have created meaning and definitions of identity which contrast with the increasing determination of individual and collective life by impersonal technocratic power. (Melucci, 1988, p. 247).

The cultural practices common within social movement spheres, ranging from the dissemination of alternative information to consciousness-raising and forms of psychotherapy, have the function for the individual that they provide alternative ideological formations and self-understanding, and for the movement that they provide a basis of solidarity and self-identification with the movement which breaks down instrumental attitudes towards mobilization and participation.

The social and cultural aspects of new social movements do supply individuals with 'incentives', but not in the narrow sense of Olson's 'selective incentives', nor Oberschall's 'rewards'.

Some incentives *are* of the Olson type. For example, new social movements provide for their 'members' alternative sources of information about a wide variety of services, ranging from consumption to psychotherapy. To take one striking example, the quickest and most reliable information on the after-effects of Chernobyl on Western Europe came not from governments, but from native ecology movements. The general level of public awareness was highest in those countries such as West Germany and Austria where these movements were most active.

Other rewards and incentives are, however, less tangible and cannot easily be accommodated within conventional resource mobilization/rational choice frameworks. This is best illustrated by a practice such as consciousness-raising. This presents individuals with an opportunity, not normally available, to reconstruct their life histories according to standards and criteria different from those of their familial socialization. Here again it is not particularly important whether the effects are real or illusory; they are probably both. What is important is the significance individuals ascribe to it.

Likewise, loose social movement spheres provide friendship networks. They guarantee the individual contact with others who are likely to share their interests and values. They provide individuals with interlocutors who are probably both more sympathetic and critical than those likely to be encountered by chance. And they present opportunities for primary social relations of friendship with less effort than is required under normal circumstances. Social movement networks have many of the advantages of clubs or voluntary associations, with the additional characteristic that the interpersonal relations may be more intense.

What is the significance of this for the mobilization of resources? Social movement networks bind the individual to the movement by creating primary bonds in which interpersonal sanction and commitment can operate. The interpersonal character of these networks minimizes problems of free-riding. Furthermore, and perhaps more fundamentally, they create self-identification with the movement. Processes of reformation of the individual will are simultaneously formations of a collective will. There is a sense in which social movement networks re-socialize the individual into different values. But the picture is more complicated than this. Group identity, not merely individual identity, is formed by the movement at the level of its loose networks. Thus Melucci is correct to emphasize that movements are not actors with given identities, and that the formation of group identity is the central sociological question.[9]

The concept of social movement networks or social movement spheres is more satisfactory than theories of resource mobilization in that it posits types of actor motivation and orientation which are richer and more varied than instrumental calculation. The informal networks provide the source of actor mobilization by creating affective social bonds and an ethic of solidarity in which, at least in part, normal instrumental rationality is suspended. It is only by focusing on the process of group formation within informal networks that we can understand how social collective action is at all possible, how an act can indeed be an end in itself, and how values of commitment can become a material force.

Melucci, like Touraine, appears to view the cultural emphasis of social movements as specific to post-industrial movements. This seems a false dichotomy, because if breaking down instrumental orientations is a pre-condition for collective action then older movements, just as much as newer ones, would have had to create a basis of solidarity and self-identification or ego involvement with the movement. Rather than suggesting that cultural activity marks new social movements from older movements I would argue that this represents a division of labour within movements. By providing individuals with alternative lifestyles and identities, social movements break down barriers to collective action, challenge 'civil privatism', and substitute values of solidarity for instrumental rationality. In other words, they undermine conditions conducive to 'free riding' and the calculation of personal benefits. The informal networks in which social movements are based challenge the 'normal' (individualistic and *zweckrational*) basis of action in everyday life and substitute affective and solidary orientations. One central point of divergence is that whereas the cultural nature of social movements is a characteristic specific to new social movements within the macro-theories, I am suggesting that it is a pre-condition for collective action as such, and therefore just as characteristic of the workers' movement as of new social movements. Thus, while group therapy and consciousness-raising may be relatively recent innovations, in building groups and group loyalty they have their functional equivalents in workers' education, and in black churches.

The notion of the social movement sector does not yet show why actors should seek alternative, collectively formed identities. The notion of a discursive formation of preferences developed by Offe and Wiesenthal, and I have suggested, implicit in Melucci, may explain why preferences can be moulded collectively once actors are involved in collective action. But it does not make clear how they came to be involved in the process of collective action and will formation. In a sense they do not get out of the dilemma posed by rational choice theories for understanding collective action, namely, why should people get involved in the first place. If we return again to Hirschman's argument, we find some interesting suggested answers to this question.

Hirschman identifies in the precommitment stage a basis on which the decision to become involved can be made intelligible. Understanding involvement requires that we address the second of the questions I identified above, namely, what is the rational basis of solidarity? Albert Hirschman's analysis of what he refers to as 'shifting involvements' tackles this question in a novel way.

Hirschman emphasizes that civil privatism, consumerism and rational calculation bring with them their own discontents; and that collective action provides, or appears to provide, an escape. Hirschman's analysis thus links exogenous and endogenous explanations of preference formation.

It is not possible here to enumerate all the discontents Hirschman identifies, but one is particularly important for this discussion. RMT-type explanations of mobilization emphasize that there is, viewed instrumentally, little direct reward for collective action. Hirschman agrees, but argues that one of the main attractions of action in the public sphere is precisely that it allows us to suspend instrumental attitudes towards actions:

One of the major attractions of public life is the exact opposite of the most fundamental characteristic of private pleasures under modern conditions: while the pursuit of the latter through the production of income (work) is clearly marked off from the eventual enjoyment of these pleasures, there is no such clear distinction at all between the pursuit of the public happiness and the attainment of it. (Hirschman, 1982, pp. 84–5).

The kind of argument Hirschman develops is analogous to claims sometimes made about the family in more familiar sociological discussions, namely, that it provides an escape from public life into relations based upon affective rather than instrumental orientations. The radical critique of family life has taught us to be wary of such idealizations (see Barrett and McIntosh, 1985), and there is no need to transfer these idealized images on to social movements. But it is not necessary for the family to be a refuge from the impersonal relations of public life for it to be viewed as such, and treated accordingly. Likewise Hirschman is arguing that collective public activity is viewed as an escape from the frustrations of civil privatism, but he is also keen to identify the frustrations built into action in the public realm.

Comparing social movement networks with the family suggests an addition to Hirschman's argument. Hirschman views collective action as a response to the disappointments of private consumption. But it may be equally valid to view collective and public action as a response to the disappointments and disaffections of family life. We can at least hope that the informal networks of primary relations within the social movement sphere may supply what we had expected from family life, but failed to receive. They also have specific advantages. For example, joining and leaving social movement networks at least appears more the result of individual volition, and there is an absence of formal and legal barriers to entrance and exit. This does not invalidate Hirschman's disenchanted view that any course of action will bring with it its own disappointments and frustration, but it does add an additional factor in the cycle.

CONCLUSION

The quite distinct, though complementary, arguments of Offe and Wiesenthal, Melucci and Hirschman suggest that we can understand the social role of movements and movement networks partly in terms of the familiar sociological notions of a search for community, primary relations, solidary values, etc. These arguments broaden and enrich our understanding of the motivations behind collective action and suggest that the barriers to such actions identified in theories of resource mobilization may be less absolute than a strictly instrumental model of action allows.

An emphasis on cultural factors modifies rather than negates theories of resource mobilizations. In the final chapter I shall argue that exclusively culturalist interpretations of social movements ignore the political and institutional dimension. Here, however, I wish to summarize some of the implications of RMT for the interpretation of social movements.

RMT draws our attention to at least one vital feature of social movements which any adequate theory must take account of, namely, it points to the inherent instability of collective action and the fact that this poses organizational and tactical problems for social movements. More specifically, the tactical dilemmas faced by social movements which rely on wide mobilization act as an incentive to lowering the costs of collective action, and this in turn pulls movements towards (i) formal organization with quasi-professional leadership; (ii) 'legitimate' institutional activity rather than 'illegitimate' – especially illegal – forms of action.

Nevertheless, theories of resource mobilization say little about the content and the socio-political context of collective action. They are concerned with the dynamics of collective action as such, independent of context and of the actual aims of such actions. If, however, we are to understand specific social movements an approach is required which situates them sociologically and politically. In the final chapter I shall argue that a middle-range theory of social movements which combines a sociological account of social closure with a political analysis of the process of 'interest intermediation' may be useful in situating social movements in their socio-political context.

6

Social closure and political participation

'. . . all the essential questions of sociology are nothing other than the questions of political science.'
Antonio Gramsci, *Prison Notebooks* p. 244

To treat the discussion of social movement sectors and of the cultural side of social movements as an attempt to address questions of mobilization is to miss much of the point of recent discussion. Defining social movements in terms of their informal network-like character is intended as a *differentia specifica* between old and new movements. Melucci, for example, criticizes interpretations of social movements which locate them within the political sphere and which imply any strong continuities between movements, pressure groups and political parties. There is thus a substantive disagreement between culturalist interpretations and theories such as resource mobilization which, as I have argued, are underpinned by political realism or pluralism.

Culturalist interpretations define social movements in life-style or sub-cultural terms. As in the case of Touraine, there is at least the implication that political movements are not 'true' social movements: 'Alain Touraine is quite reluctant to define the Peace movement as a social movement, because it is based essentially on a critical attitude towards the state' (Meier, 1988, p. 80). Political movements are equated with workers' movements and hence with industrial society; movements in post-industrial society are not thought to be of this type.

This exclusion is arbitrary in presupposing one ideal type to which all movements should conform, but few in fact actually do. Civil rights movements, and aspects of broader movements concerned with civil rights, protest movements such as the peace movement, ecology as far as it is concerned with either opposing state planning or in party building, etc., are all excluded on the culturalist definition. In brief, new movements *are* concerned with issues many of which can be thematized in terms of civil rights and citizenship, and thus make political demands whether for resources or legislative and legal changes.

Likewise, Hirschman's argument treats collective action too exclusively as a public solution to private problems, albeit private problems which have their origins in a social malaise. But looking at movements in this way fails to address the question of why particular movements are viewed by individuals as legitimate expressions of their concerns and interests, and as being worthy of support. Basic to the argument of this chapter is the view that if we confine analysis of social movements to the cultural sphere, we shall fail to develop a realistic assessment of their likely effects.

Contrary to culturalist interpretations, no categorical distinction can be drawn between social movements, pressure groups and parties. Social movements are best understood in terms of a continuum stretching from informal network-like associations to formal party-like organizations. We can realistically assess the effects of social movements upon their environment only, by viewing them as a political phenomenon related to other more 'institutional' expressions of political interests. It is thus necessary for the sociological interpretation of social movements to return to the realist, and if necessary pluralist, models of political action and interest representation. On the other hand, theories of mobilization are by themselves too limiting. Confining explanation to processes of mobilization fails to address two central questions about social movements generally: (i) What is the social base and aim of collective action? (ii) What are the criteria of social movement 'success'? It also fails to address the central question of theories of new social movements in particular, namely: Wherein lies the 'newness' of new movements?

In sum, approaches which fail to incorporate the cultural aspects of social movements cannot account for mobilization and normative innovation; approaches which confine themselves to cultural/life-style aspects fail to offer a realistic assessment of movement aims and possible effects.

In what follows I shall argue for an accommodation of culturalist and political explanations of collective action and social movement effects. It may be useful first to clarify schematically an ideal-type model of what I have called 'realist' and 'culturalist' theories.

Table 6.1 Competing characterizations of social movements

	Realist	Culturalist
Location	state	civil society
Aims	political/cultural integration	innovation/defence
Movement orientation	institutional	non/anti-institutional
Actor orientation	instrumental	self-identification

c.f. J.A. Hannigan, 1985, p. 436

The differences represented in the table hide two important similarities: first, both models treat the social and political as discrete; second, they confine social movements a priori to either civil society or to the political sphere. The division between social and political movements is particularly important in the macro-theories of social movements because it is thought to correspond to the historical division between old and new movements. In contrast I shall argue that the social/political distinction is common to new and old social movements and that it corresponds not to a division between movements, but to a division of functions within them. This does not imply that all movements are political – exceptions may include religious movements, moral crusades, etc. – but it does imply that all political movements are social in the sense intended by theorists such as Touraine and Melucci. The characteristics imputed to new social movements by these theorists are, however, generalizable to older movements. Conversely, many new movements are political in the sense intended by the alternative resource mobilization approach, that is, concerned with political access and integration, and not confined to civil society and the re-formation of individual and collective wills, values, and life-styles.

Arguing for an accommodation of these two models implies that they are not strictly competing even if this is how they have usually been viewed, and view themselves. The two perspectives are trying to explain distinct but complementary phenomena. Culturalist theories are explanations of the *formation of interests and actors' identity* on the one hand, and *cultural and normative innovations* on the other. It is the weakness of theories of resource mobilization and political realism that they fail to account for preference formation and cultural/normative innovation. Nevertheless realist approaches do address a question that the macro-level culturalist perspectives tackle inadequately, namely, *the way social movements achieve their effects*. Culturalist theories do have a partial explanation of social movements effects in terms of cultural innovation, but because they disregard political negotiation they fail to analyse the processes by which such cultural innovations are fed into politics, how new political agendas become set, and how political parties, pressure groups, etc., react to external pressure. Without an understanding of processes of interests intermediation, as well as formation, we shall fail to produce a realistic assessment of the nature and extent of social movement effects.

The limitations of both micro-level explanations of mobilization and culturalist definitions of movements can be overcome by supplementing these approaches with a sociological theory of social closure on the one hand, and a political theory of interest intermediation on the other.[1] I shall illustrate this argument through a discussion of 'corporatism'. This is useful for a number of reasons: first, it is in the debate around corporatism that we find a non-pluralist theory of interest intermediation; second, the corporatist approach locates the political context of some forms of recent social movements; finally, such theories are compatible with sociological accounts of social closure.

SOCIAL CLOSURE, EXCLUSION AND
INTEREST INTERMEDIATION

Social Closure

The Weberian term 'closure' describes the processes by which groups come to be formed through strategies of inclusion and exclusion. Following Weber, Parkin defines closure as 'the process by which social collectivities seek to maximize rewards by restricting access to resources and opportunities to a limited circle of eligibles' (1979, p. 44). The activity of social movements, though they also include processes of closure in this sense, typically represent the opposite side of this process: they are attempts by groups thus excluded to insert themselves into closed groups, and into closed processes of negotiation between groups; and by so doing to gain access to new resources and opportunities. Parkin refers to this latter tactic as 'usurpation', but 'insertion' or 'inclusion' would appear more satisfactory since modern social movements tend to thematize inclusion in processes of decision-making and in citizenship rights rather than the direct usurpation of power.

In contrast to macro-level identification of the aims of social movements which exclude the political forms of activity, a middle-range theory of social closure enables us to identify the two central types of social movement activity: first, the expansion of citizenship; and second, the insertion of excluded groups into the polity.[2] These aspects of social movement activity reflect their two major projects: social movements articulate the grievances and demands of (i) groups who are excluded from the benefits typically available to average citizens, or (ii) those who are excluded from established elite groupings and from processes of elite negotiation. It is thus useful to distinguish not merely revolutionary from non-revolutionary social movements, but also, among the latter, movements of social citizenship and movements of political integration. This distinction is not categorical. Clearly ethnic minorities, for example, who do not enjoy the citizenship rights typically available to members of society are also excluded from power, and any social movement expressing their concerns will have to address both aspects.

Both citizenship movements and movements of political

integration make demands of the state, but the demands are of a different type. Citizenship movements make claims on resources and on the extension of rights already available to other citizens. Their demands will normally be articulated in the language of *rights*. Movements of political participation, on the other hand, likewise make claims on resources, but in addition make claims to inclusion in processes of political decision-making. Their demands are typically articulated in the language of *participation*.

Locating social movements in terms of social closure is incompatible with the types of macro-theories discussed earlier because it assumes that the central theme/aim of movements is integration. I shall return to these differences in the final section. Here I wish to argue that sociological accounts of closure are not necessarily incompatible with all theories of long-term social change. This point can be illustrated through a brief consideration of some aspects of Gellner's analysis of nationalism.

Gellner interprets the rise of nationalism against the background of a long-term theory of social change which focuses on the transition from agrarian to industrial society. He identifies the central characteristics of industrial society as: (i) production based upon knowledge: 'Work, in the main, is no longer the manipulation of things, but of meanings' (Gellner, 1983, pp. 32–3); (ii) as a precondition for this, 'high culture' is progressively disseminated throughout society. This has implications for the central institutions of industrial society. Not merely a high level of education, but also cultural homogeneity based upon shared knowledge and culture characterizes industrial societies. Culture, as Gellner notes, is 'no longer an adornment', but rather the 'necessary shared medium, the life blood or perhaps rather the minimal shared atmosphere, within which alone members of the society can breathe and survive and produce' (1983, pp. 37–8). Through this process general non-specialized education is the pivot of a society in which 'monopoly of legitimate education is now more important, more central than is the monopoly of legitimate violence' (1983, p. 34).

Gellner's analysis differs from those considered in chapter 3 in a number of respects. His characterization of industrial society as being grounded in the knowledge-based production of meaning is similar to Touraine's characterization of post-industrial society, with the following exception, and which is crucial. For Gellner this is a feature of industrial society as such, and he posits no qualitative break between industrial and post-industrial society. This avoids the technological reductionism implied in the assumption that manufacture is an extended form of physical labour. Paradoxically, given Gellner's highly critical attitude towards Marxism, his analysis is in many respects more 'materialist' than that of Touraine, who is ultimately a technological reductionist, or Habermas, who views the development of modern society in terms of the disembodied Weberian concept of 'rationalization'. In contrast to both, the agents of the spread of nationalism Gellner identifies are *classes*, if not in the classical Marxist sense of owners or non-owners of the means of production, then at least in the sense that their social position is identified in terms of their position in productive processes, and their monopoly over one central means of production: knowledge.

The long-term stages theory of history which Gellner proposes is not of interest here. None the less, there are features of his explanation which shed light on the preconditions for social movement activity in general and are compatible with explanations in terms of social closure. Within the context of the developmental argument Gellner identifies nationalism as an ideology which allows groups hitherto excluded from privilege by the mechanisms of colonialism to develop a collective identity:

> The cultural/linguistic distance and capacity to differentiate themselves from others, which is such a handicap for individuals, can be and often is eventually a positive advantage for entire collectivities, or potential collectivities, of these victims of the newly emerging world. (Gellner, 1983, p. 62).

Furthermore, nationalist ideology is for Gellner first and foremost an ideology of and for relatively privileged and highly educated sections within culturally and linguistically under-privileged populations. It enables this section of society both to articulate the injustice of their arbitrary exclusion, and to develop a comprehensible ideology of appeal to their entire ethnic group.

In these two aspects of Gellner's analysis lie clues to understanding aspects of the so-called new social movements within Western society. The analogy with Gellner's analysis of nationalism is relevant here in two respects: first, with regard to the social basis of new movements' members; second, with regard to the issue of exclusion and closure. I shall return to the latter point in the discussion of corporatism; here I wish to consider the similarity between the social base of new social movements and Gellner's analysis of nationalism.

New social movements are typically either predominantly movements of the educated middle classes, especially the 'new middle class', or of the most educated/privileged section of generally less privileged groups.

The first type of case is well illustrated again by Green movements and parties in Western Europe. As Müller-Rommel notes, 'Several studies confirm that green party voters are well-educated young citizens, members of the new middle class, usually employed in the non-productive white-collar service sector of the economy and the state bureaucracy' (1985b, pp. 493–4). He also notes that even among the young and better educated, it is those in urban areas who are most likely to vote Green and involve themselves in the 'new politics'. Other political scientists characterize this section of society as a 'third generation': highly educated but lacking power and thus having distinct interests:

> The children of normal politics today are therefore open to both new ideologies and new parties if these support new answers to questions of political and individual density. If, in political situations in which the ties between the youngest cohorts and the established parties are weakest, the present economic situation and the future expectations of these cohorts are frustrated by party programmes, the possibility of realignment to parties that will better represent these interests increases. (Bürklin, 1985, pp. 477–8).

It is the paradoxical position of this 'third generation' – on the one hand relatively privileged, on the other hand excluded from processes of political negotiation – rather than any absolute disadvantage which may account for their tendency towards new forms of political ideology and expression. Here the analogy with Gellner's analysis is particularly striking. Exclusion as such is not a sufficient condition for attraction to new forms of politics. As Gellner points out, there are many more potential than actual nationalisms. What is important is rather the paradoxical situation of members of the new middle classes, particularly the young. In the terminology of the French sociologist Pierre Bourdieu, such groups are high in 'cultural' and 'educational' capital, but have relatively restricted access to processes of political decision-making.

At least in terms of their social base, new social movements are class movements in Gellner's extended Weberian sense. The class nature of new movements is recognized by analysts such as Claus Offe for whom 'New middle-class politics is, in contrast to most working-class politics as well as old middle-class politics, typically a politics of a class, but not on behalf of a class' (Offe, 1987, p. 77). I think that the distinction being made here is difficult to defend, not because the new politics is reducible to class interest, but because the relationship between class interest and political practice is probably more complicated in all the cases Offe mentions. Working-class politics makes its appeal to universal standards of justice and fairness just as ecological politics appeals to humanity and a humanized nature as a universal ethic. The new politics, like the old, has a double face: it is both of and on behalf of classes, but appeals to more than class interest. One thing illustrated in the discussion of corporatism, including Offe's, is that the new politics give expression to the frustrations of the new middle class precisely because they identify and articulate a set of issues excluded from mainstream political negotiation.

While analysis in these broadly class/generational terms may identify the broad social base of new social movement activity, we need a more concrete political analysis in order to locate such movements within social and political processes. It is here that recent discussion of interest intermediation and corporatism is useful.

Political intermediation

At the level of concrete political analysis new social movements, especially those which have taken on an overtly political form, can be viewed as a reaction to the failure of the institutions of interest intermediation: parliaments, the media and, especially, political parties.

This type of claim for social movements raises the spectre of pluralism, and slips back into the type of institutional analysis to which the theory of social movements is often taken to be an alternative. The resistance sociological theories of social movements have shown to existing accounts of political intermediation stems from the critique of the institutional approaches associated with pluralist political analysis. - The rejection of the assumptions of pluralism, repeated by Castells even in his post-Althusserian writings (see Castells, 1983, chapter 28), have highlighted weaknesses in pluralism: its failure to accommodate structural power, its blindness to agenda setting, its assumption of a rough equality of access, etc.[4]

The problem with the critique of pluralism is not that it is not well grounded, but rather that it has led to a systematic neglect of those issues which pluralism addresses, on the assumption that their significance is limited to the pluralist paradigm or problematic. Thus, although sophisticated Marxist theories of the state recognize the (partial) independence of the state from class relations, the focus of concern has remained on the state's role in the reproduction of capital/labour relation and capital accumulation, and not with the processes by which interests in civil society are fed into the polity. As Philippe Schmitter has noted:

> By defining the state as a unitary actor and endowing it with both a responsibility and a capacity for guaranteeing the long-run reproductive imperatives of capitalism, the demands and protestations of existing social classes and their 'fractions', even those of bourgeois beneficiaries from state largesse and protection, can be dismissed. (Schmitter, 1979, p. 89).

In the case of social movements the effect is to distract attention away from the specific political context of their activity. Both the citizenship-type and the political integrative-type of social movements identified above are concerned to make claims on the state and to feed their demands into the polity. By restricting social movements to the sphere of civil society and culture one vital causal precondition is bypassed: the failure of institutions of political intermediation to take new political demands on board and to accommodate the interests of certain central social groups.

Furthermore, neglecting political processes has meant that sociological theories of social movements fail to account for the form movement activity has taken in the political arena. It has thus been largely left to political scientists to point to the significance of the existing 'political opportunity structures' in shaping the course of social movement strategy and success or failure (see Kitschelt, 1985). These political factors are nevertheless important because they provide a link between the more general sociological preconditions – the growth of the new middle classes, etc. – on the one hand, and the more specific political preconditions on the other.

The question for a theory of social movements which neither wishes to ignore the political nor assume a straightforward pluralism is how to develop an account of political intermediation along non-pluralist lines. Again we may look towards corporatist theory for some suggestions here. Streeck and Schmitter (1985) in particular have been concerned to develop a non-pluralist theory of interest intermediation: a theory which recognizes the importance of the civil society/polity relation, but without presupposing that the political system offers an undistorted 'reflection' of societal interests, or equality between different interest groups.

Streeck and Schmitter have radicalized a theory of interest intermediation into a general theory of 'private interest government' and an 'associational' model of the social order: 'a corporative-associative order is . . . based primarily on interaction within and between interdependent complex organizations' (1985, p. 10). Within associational social orders the aim of the state is to 'satisfy interests' (p. 13). Corporatist theorists thus recognize the centrality of associational-type institutions which mediate between state and civil society. More radically, such analysis calls any strict state/civil society distinction into question. This would clearly have implications for the theory of social movements not least because it would no longer be possible to define them as non-political in the manner of the dominant sociological paradigm. But the discussion of corporatism is also significant in drawing attention to the importance of the processes through which interests become aggregated and articulated at least in societies in which associational processes are central. This is the theme which recent analysts of social movements have picked up, and which I suggest is vital to understanding the significance of new movements and to locating them neither in civil society nor the state, but in the interface between state and civil society.

Both Claus Offe and Birgitta Nedelmann have recently identified processes of political intermediation and the state/civil society relation as central to an understanding of mobilization (Nedelmann) and the political significance of new movements (Offe). In Nedelmann's analysis political parties are viewed as vital, if flawed, means of transmitting individual demands into the processes of political decision-making. In the absence of parties which can perform this function satisfactorily, social movements provide an alternative means for actors to aggregate and articulate interests and demands: 'Action-groups, ad hoc groups, social movements and other loosely structured organizations have taken over the role of mobilizing individuals' (Nedelmann, 1987, p. 182).

Offe's analysis develops a similar theme with respect to the failure of mass parties to remain in touch with their base, and to political decision-making to apply instrumental technocratic criteria. For Offe, modern political parties are caught in a dilemma created by the mechanisms of representative democracy. To succeed in electoral democracies, parties must broaden their appeal and adopt mass party (*Volkspartei*) models. This entails an increasing distance of parties from their original social base, or indeed from an unambiguous identification with the interests of any particular section of society. Moreover, politics itself is reduced to a means of producing effective 'outputs' according to largely instrumental standards. At the same time, Offe, in common with most West German analysts, still views new movements as qualitatively different from the workers' movement and identifies old and new 'paradigms' of political activity:

> The new social movements seek to politicize civil society in ways that are not constrained by representative-bureaucratic political institutions and thereby to reconstitute a civil society independent from increasing control and intervention. To emancipate itself from the state, the new movements claim, civil society itself – its institutions, and its very standards of rationality and progress – must employ practices that belong to an intermediate sphere between private pursuits and concerns and institutional, state-sanctioned modes of politics (Offe, 1987, p. 65).

Again, in so far as all social movements are concerned to effect social change they are bound to argue for new unconventional practices and politicize areas of activity previously thought of as personal; this applies just as much to the workers' movement's insistence on the political nature of the employment contract as it does to the politicization of gender relations, etc. Furthermore, analysing social movement activity in terms of political intermediation and the mobilization of interests in the way Nedelmann, and indeed Offe, do, suggests a continuity in the nature of social movement activity, though this does not imply that the issues remain the same.

In the following discussion I shall argue that corporatist theorists and critics have identified the political context of much recent social movement activity. Their analysis is also interesting in that it identifies important characteristics of the political environment in which movements operate. It is particularly in the more corporatist-type political arrangements that movements of political integration are most prevalent, or in which citizenship-type movements are more likely to develop into participatory movements. To illustrate this point I wish to refer once again to the case of environmental movements in Western Europe.

In the case of Western European Green parties we can see how an explanation in terms of social closure may help us understand the social and political context of new social movement activity. It helps to explain one central characteristic, namely, why these movements have been strongest in countries where neo-corporatist political arrangements have characterized political decision-making processes, and where dualist or free market options have not been adopted, at least not to the extent that they have in Britain. The critique of the closed nature of the political system has largely been made in the context of, and with reference to these countries – namely, Sweden, West Germany and Austria. These are also among the countries in which ecological movements have been most active in the political sphere. What is it about neo-corporatist arrangements that has stimulated the development of Green movements in those countries?

Corporatism's critics have identified several aspects of this type of political decision-making process which may have stimulated the development of non class-based oppositional movements. They have pointed to the technocratic character of political decision-making in which the agenda has been stable over extended periods of time, and in which debate is stifled under a real or apparent consensus. The Austrian political scientist Anton Pelinka uses the vivid phrase *Scheinkonflikt* (the tendency towards the appearance of conflict) (1980, p. 25) to characterize the bloodless nature of political debate in societies where political choice is largely reduced to a choice of 'management styles', and in which elite negotiation is conducted by a small group of 'social partners' who are familiar both with each other and with the fixed set of rules surrounding their negotiations.

In contrast to dualism, corporatist arrangements are normally characterized as 'inclusive', that is, as incorporating groups in negotiation. Its critics point out that the negotiating 'partners' are restricted, in large part, to employers and organized labour. Even with respect to the latter there are limitations. Unions in traditional 'core' manufacturing sectors – typically metal industries – are over-represented at the expense of, for example, white collar and service unions. Immigrant and women workers, largely to be found in service industries, are likewise under-represented in processes of corporate negotiation. Thus inclusion of some entails exclusion of others, and corporatism is not irreconcilable with dualist elements. Particularly in highly institutionalized forms of corporatism, peak level negotiation consists of negotiation between a highly restricted elite who hold multiple office, and have close personal ties with those on the other side of the table.

Corporatist forms of elite negotiation have precipitated new forms of protest for a number of reasons. First, formal democratic procedures are largely circumvented by negotiation between the partners which takes place behind the back of formally democratic institutions. This has narrowly circumscribed the range of debate within parliament, between parties, and in the media. Similarly, union dissent has been limited by, or according to left critics thwarted by, the pressure on already hierarchical union organizations to 'deliver' on their promises by imposing discipline on their members.

Second, the closed, and closely circumscribed, nature of political decision-making means that groups excluded from these processes may mobilize at grass-roots level, knowing that 'normal' channels are closed off. This is particularly the case for important social groupings who find themselves outside processes of elite negotiation, and above all for the growing middle class, especially in the service sector, the so-called new middle class. It is the paradoxical position of the new middle class, rather than its exclusion alone, which has inclined it towards social protest and ecological ideology. The social partners within corporatist arrangements have been largely restricted to representatives of capital and labour, and in particular labour in traditional manufacturing industries such as steel, coal and chemicals. Within corporatist arrangements these groups retain a degree of political power at a time when they have become economically less significant, with the decline of these industries and of the proportion of the population employed in them. At the same time, white collar workers, particularly those in the tertiary sector, have been growing in number and economic importance, but have remained nevertheless at the periphery of corporatist decision-making.

This suggests that ecology has become a possible ideology of the new middle classes in countries which have retained corporatist political arrangements. What is it about ecological issues and arguments that is attractive to this social group? Two factors are significant here. First, ecology has identified many of the undesirable unintended consequences of industrialism which corporatist arrangements serve to reinforce; second, it has been generalizable into an ideological critique of industrial society as such, and particularly the features of industrial society which have caused the new middle classes to feel especially aggrieved, namely, the political domination of the heavy manufacturing industry. Thus ecological ideas identify issues which are systematically excluded from corporatist negotiations, and provide an intellectual critique of both industrial society and traditional labourist politics.

Corporatism is premised on sustained economic growth, and high levels of employment. Therefore, corporatist 'solutions' to differences of class interest, even or especially where they are successful, displace social and economic 'crises' on to environmental pressures. This is especially so in cases where governments subsidize building projects (for example, power stations, or road building) in the absence of a market demand in order to inhibit unemployment trends and maintain the state's part of the bargain. In these cases it becomes difficult to explain to citizens the necessity of such projects given the manifest environmental damage which they entail.

Austria in particular has provided examples of strong popular resistance to such plans both in the sphere of nuclear energy, where a referendum in 1978 put a seemingly permanent halt to the country's nuclear energy programme, and conventional power station projects, as is the case with the planned hydro-electric plant on the Danube east of Vienna (Hainburg, stopped in 1984).

The problem of rational justification for such major government projects is made more difficult by a further apparent by-product of closed elite negotiation within a corporatist framework, namely, corruption. This is illustrated most dramatically, in the Austrian case, by the corruption scandal of the late 1970s, which dragged on into the late 1980s, of the building of a major general hospital in Vienna. In the West German case the scandal surrounding the property development plans of the '*Neue Heimat*' (a union-owned housing association) in West Berlin provides a strikingly similar example.

This explanation of the relationship between corporatism and ecological movements which has been developed by corporatism's left and libertarian critics, and by the movements themselves, does, I think, help situate the rise of Green movements in Europe in their political context. However, there are problems with such an explanation, and it needs to be modified in a number of respects.

If the first place, although corporatism has adhered to an ideology of growth and has thus contributed to the creation of the secondary dysfunctions of industrialism such as pollution and excessive major building projects, countries such as Britain which have adopted free market politics have similarly remained committed to economic growth, and are at least equally insensitive to its possible secondary dysfunctions. Corporatism must thus have other characteristics than those indicated by its critics which have stimulated the development of Green movements. Furthermore, the exclusion of large numbers of citizens from decision-making is not restricted to corporatism. Continental ecology movements have been somewhat ethnocentric in their critique.

Exclusion and growth ideology are not then sufficient conditions for the development of Green movements in Western Europe. The politicized nature and transparency of decision-making processes within corporatism, and the centrality of class have been further key background conditions for the development of European ecology. But in addition corporatist structures may present social movements with sets of political opportunities which incline them to adopt political forms. For example, the strong group/class identification (what Pelinka calls '*Lagerdenken*' – thinking in camps) facilitated by corporatist arrangements may encourage the formation of new groupings. At the same time systems of proportional representation and state subsidies for political parties may channel activities into a party political form. Thus it may be the co-existence of inclusive and exclusionary factors rather than, as corporatism's critics have tended to emphasize, exclusion alone which may account for the development of new parties in countries like Austria and West Germany.

Furthermore, while the secondary dysfunctions of industrialism may be no less apparent in free market economics than they are in corporatist ones, in the latter case it is also possible to identify the agents, both institutionally and individually, responsible. Many cases of large-scale pollution and certainly major building projects are the outcomes of political decision-making processes, and identifiably the result of negotiation between social partners. The first part at least of this statement is true also of road building, nuclear power station building, etc., in non-corporatist countries. But here too, the public projects which were the outcome of public decision-making have been the most controversial. Nevertheless, it is the second factor – the intimacy of the link between individual projects and corporatist negotiation – which has served to sharpen conflict. Austria's attempted nuclear programme referred to above is a case in point. One ground for resisting the programme was the public awareness that the fundamental motivation has been the maintenance of the social partnership through the creation of new major building projects rather than actual energy requirements.

The effects of corporatism may thus be more paradoxical than its critics suggest. On the one hand, many 'political' issues are rubber-stamped in the absence of a genuine public debate, but on the other hand, it is difficult to appeal to the market's hidden hand in justifying decisions, or in explaining economic developments. Issues may be de-politicized in the sense that consensus acts as a dead hand on debate, but at the same time they remain political decisions and negotiation. To this extent Habermas's characterization of modern capitalist society as one in which economic relations are politicized is appropriate at least as a description of the politicizing effects of corporatism.

In addition to the politicized and relatively transparent nature of corporatism's decision-making processes, the fact that they are based on class negotiation has also been important for the development of new social movements. Here too the effects of corporatism have been paradoxical. As Goldthorpe points out against both liberals and corporatism's Marxist critics '[corporatism] tends rather to endow class – as opposed to group – interests with a new significance' (1984, p. 327). More specifically, the classes in question have been the major ones in industrial capitalist society: capital and labour. Corporatism has excluded not merely non-class interest groups from decision-making, but other classes, notably the new middle class.

I have discussed the corporatist nature of much new social movement activity not because such movements are confined to corporatist contexts, but because this is the context which appears to encourage political manifestations of social movement activity most and this has been neglected in sociological accounts of new movements; also the debate around corporatism draws out some wider implications for the analysis of social movements. It illustrates the usefulness of theories of social closure in understanding social movements' formation and aims. It also is an illustration of how the institutional constraints *and* opportunities can shape the form and direction of social movement activity. Conversely, we may assume that the absence of such constraints and opportunities affects the form and strength of social movements under more dualist political arrangements. One task for a sociological understanding of social movements is to connect broader developmental factors with the kinds of analysis political scientists have developed of the shaping of interest articulation by institutional and political factors.

IMPLICATIONS OF MIDDLE-RANGE THEORIES OF SOCIAL MOVEMENTS

I should like finally to enumerate some of the implications of a middle-range theory of new social movements. This type of approach affects our understanding of the nature and significance of social movements in a two key ways: first, how we understand their aims, define the criteria of their success or failure, and understand their role in bringing about social change; second, how we identify the 'newness' of new social movements:

Aims and criteria of success

The macro-theories of social movements discussed earlier assume that the aim of social movements, or at least true social movements, is the creation of alternative societies which challenge the status quo *in toto*. This reduces social movements to (i) their most fundamentalist expressions, and (ii) their cultural aspects. In contrast, viewing social movements as challenges to social closure suggests quite a different aim and criterion of success, namely, integration.

The argument here is that the aims of social movements can be defined in terms of their challenge to processes of social closure and exclusion. Social movements are agents of social change but not, as their theorists often suggest, necessarily or usually of total social transformation. Social movements typically bring about change, or attempt to bring it about, not by challenging society as a whole, though they may appear to do so, but by opposing specific forms of social closure and exclusion. They do so by thematizing issues excluded from normal societal and political decision-making, and by articulating the grievances of groups who are themselves excluded. These two aspects – exclusion of issues and exclusion of groups – are not separate spheres of social movement activity.

This actually inverts the assumptions of macro-theories of social movements. In such theories integration is equated with failure and the disappearance of the movement. The view here is that while integration does typically mean the disappearance of the movement as movement, it is at the same time the criterion of the movement's success. In practice such 'disappearance' of social movements is often only partial or temporary, since integration of issues and social groups is seldom complete, and the attainment of specific aims creates new demands. The disappearance, or dormancy, of the women's movement after the political franchise had been won, and its reappearance with new demands during the 1970s illustrates both the 'partial' nature of political integration, and also how this very success highlighted other forms of discrimination and exclusion, giving rise to new demands and analyses.

Equating failure and integration is the result of a fetishized view of social movements: the view that 'the movement is everything', an end in itself. But this is to give priority to the means over the ends. At the same time these interpretations of social movements polarize change and integration in such a way that real change is equated with qualitative shifts in the boundary conditions of the social system, and integration is equated with incorporation. This dichotomy – change or integration – is, perhaps ironically, shared by strictly pluralist analyst and many left analysts of social movements and political processes. It is illustrated in Papadakis's analysis of the West German Greens. Papadakis quotes Klanderman's, and Tarrow's statement that conventional politics is 'the continuation of non-conventional politics by other means'. He goes on to comment that 'this argument can easily exaggerate the "ordinariness" of protest politics. It overlooks how they challenge and extend the boundaries of conventional politics and contribute to the "transformation of political culture"' (Papadakis, 1988, p. 439). But Papadakis's criticism assumes the polarization of conventional and non-conventional politics: either change or integration. In contrast, viewing social movements as a challenge to social closure stresses, and this seems to me the real import of Klanderman's and Tarrow's observation, that integration is social and political change. It is the integration, and 'normalization', of previously excluded, and 'exotic' issues such as ecology into mainstream politics that constitutes a fundamental shift in the character of conventional politics. Without this integration these issues would remain marginal. This is not to side with the purely integrationist assumptions of pluralism, but rather with the political analysis of the Realo wing of the German Greens, who welcome the shift of 'established' parties towards the issues they thematize.

The dualistic view of radical change versus incorporation is not helpful in identifying social movement effects. Political decision-making has to be opened up. Previously exotic issues become mainstream political questions, new styles of political activity have to be accepted as normal, or at least be tolerated. Culturalist interpretations, such as Touraine's, interpret the anti-nuclear movement as partial because it makes demands of the State rather than attempting to become the core of a totalizing oppositional movement within civil society. For us, its significance as a social movement is not the fact that it focuses opposition to the 'programmed society' as a whole but that it makes energy a political issue, challenging the contention that this is a technical matter better left to experts.

It may be argued that social movements effect change largely through influencing existing institutions of political intermediation, particularly political parties. It is the impact of the 'new politics' on parties which may prove in the long term the crucial mechanism of integration of new issues and groupings into mainstream politics. In particular, by articulating new issues and by forming the new middle class into a political public, ecology has provided left-of-centre parties with an opportunity to modernize their political programmes.

Such a development is illustrated by the career of the West German politician Oskar Lafontaine. Lafontaine came to prominence within the SPD because of his success in Saarland, where he developed a political platform combining left social democratic politics with ideas influenced by the West German Green Party. For politicians such as Lafontaine the possibility of political success lies not in adopting new politics wholesale, but in synthesizing them with the traditional concerns of workers' parties. Thus Lafontaine supported the demand by IG-Metall (the West German metal workers' union) for a shortening of the working week as a means of modernizing and widening union demands and policies.[4]

In sum, an analysis of social movements in terms of social closure and interest intermediation treats the integration of issues and groups into the polity as the criterion of social movement success. It thus implies that the continued existence of the movement is not an end in itself, because social movement activity can only be understood in the context of other forms of political expression, both institutionalized and non-institutionalized.

The 'newness' of new social movements

An interpretation of social movements as primarily concerned with challenging processes of social closure and exclusion affects how we understand the 'newness' of new social movements, or indeed whether we want to define them as new in any qualitative sense.

General theories of social movements attempt to identity this newness by referring to changes at the level of the social system or structure. New social movements are assumed to 'reflect' broader societal developments such as the shift of focus within the economic base from production to reproduction (Castells); industrial to post-industrial society (Touraine); or from liberal to late capitalism (Habermas). It is argued that these structural developments have thrown up qualitatively new forms of opposition within society.

On this basis, specific characteristics are imputed to new social movements which are thought to distinguish them categorically from the workers' movement. No such categorical distinction exists on the basis of structural criteria.

One *differentia specifica* of new social movements is held to be the 'non-negotiable' character of their demands and ideologies. This view assumes that capitalist society has rendered the demands of the workers' movement negotiable through their incorporation into processes of political decision-making. This has been a bone of contention within the corporatist debate, where Marxist critics such as Panitch have viewed corporatist arrangements as a means of de-radicalizing the working class, the other commentators have insisted that the role of class is reinforced rather than diminished by the existence of corporatism (see Goldthorpe, 1984, and Korpi, 1983). The former of these propositions is assumed in attempts to define new social movements by the non-negotiability of their demands. New social movements, in contrast to class-based movements, are assumed to make demands which cannot be accommodated within industrial society.

There are two further proposed means for defining new social movements: (i) their loose organizational structures, (ii) their interest in participatory democracy rather than merely the outputs of the political system. These linked characteristics are seen as specific features of these movements, distinguishing them from older ones. Loose network-type organization is thought to replace hierarchical organization, and an interest in participation to supersede an interest only in the outcome of political decision-making.

The issue here is not whether these are accurate characterizations of new social movements, but whether they identity characteristics specific to those movements alone. There are a number of problems with the argument that they do. First, such a definition of new social movements is plausible only so long as one equates the movement as a whole with its fundamentalist wing for whom movement ideology is, to use Weber's term, an ethic of absolute ends (*Gesinnungsethik*); it refuses to interact with established political institutions other than instrumentally, and equates formal organization a priori with the repressive structures of established parties and institutions. Second, the attempt to identify a *differentia specifica* on structural grounds alone reduces the social movement to one specific stage of its development, namely, the initial stage. This has all the optimism of a new movement grounded in recent mobilization, before the movement must reflect upon how it is to affect the social and political environment. Once social movements adopt strategic forms of action to achieve their goals they face organizational problems which pull them towards more conventional forms (see chapter 5). Furthermore, their goals become negotiable as they are drawn into the political process. Were goals to remain non-negotiable movements would be left with little more than the hope for a cultural revolution in values. To build non-negotiability and indifference towards the state into the definition of new social movements is to define them as exclusively cultural movements.

None of the imputed characteristics are confined to new social movements. An emphasis upon democracy and participation, for example, can be viewed as a function of the concern of social movements in general to open up social and political decision-making procedures; it is part of the rhetoric of populism. Participatory demands and ideology belong to the ideological baggage of any movement, the workers' movement just as much as new social movements, which are not yet integrated into decision-making processes, but which would dearly like to be. We cannot take this characteristic of social movements as either unique to specific types of movement, as Habermas does, nor as evidence of the essential and non-negotiable character of new social movement demands. It is only in the subsequent course of social movement development that it becomes clear which demands, if any, are truly non-negotiable, and whether or not the movement is interested in political outcomes.

A further example of the generalizability of the characteristics imputed to new social movements is the near universality of the fundamentalist/pragmatist tension. This is not confined to so-called new social movements, but is a re-expression of the division between revolutionary and social democratic tactics within the workers' movements. It is a dilemma faced by all movements once they are past their early stages of development: whether to adhere to the initial aims which clearly define the movement's uniqueness, or whether to make those aims negotiable in the hope of attaining at least some of them.

Thus attempts to identify at structural level criteria which distinguish new from previous social movements rest upon a static sociological analysis in two senses. First, such approaches are ahistorical in their exaggeration of the differences between new social movements and the workers' movement; and, second, they reify the early stage of social movement development by equating it with the movement as a whole. In this way social movements are reduced to their ideological self-representations and to their most fundamentalist manifestations.

Viewing social movements in terms of the integration of groups and issues suggests that the new social movements are 'new' only in an attenuated sense. They articulate new issues and their social base lies within the new middle class, but we cannot characterize them as 'new' in the qualitative sense implicit, and explicit, in much of the discussion around them. New movements carry on the project of older movements in a vital respect: they open up the political sphere, they articulate popular demands and they politicize issues previously confined to the private realm.

The view of social movements for which I have been arguing stresses their 'ordinariness'. Even non-institutionalized forms of action are to be understood in the context of wider institutional-ized political processes. This robs new social movements not of their significance, but of much of their novelty. We cannot rest an entire theory of social transformation upon their presence, nor look to social movements alone as harbingers of some new society. In contrast to broader sociological approaches, I have argued for an essentially 'revisionist' interpretation, and have suggested that the search for some over-arching movement is fruitless given the diversity of demands and interests. This is a view perhaps disappointingly close to a 'common-sense' understanding. But should a sociological interpretation of social movements be motivated exclusively by the search for novelty?

Notes

1 New social movements – major themes

1 What I shall call the 'culturalist' approach is common in sociological commentary in new social movements. Its main characteristic is an emphasis on changes in life-style and relationships rather than political demands and political change. The following is a typical example:

> If only those actions whose aims should be binding for the whole of society (that is, as laws) have a political quality, then such an approach fails to account for those movements and efforts which try to realize a new way of living not via the state (whether actual, 'revolutionary', or post-revolutionary state), but via the individual and society through personal transformation, new forms of relationships, a new culture (in the widest sense). (Nelles, 1984, p. 429).

Or, more straightforwardly, 'What is problematic is not political emancipation or economic justice, but subjective individual happiness and "the good life"' (Eder, 1982, p. 11). The obvious question begged by such interpretations is, 'How is the "good life" to be achieved without political emancipation or economic justice?'

2 A recent discussion of the concept of citizenship can be found in Turner, 1986. Turner argues that struggles over citizenship constitute a central feature of social relations which has been ignored, or at least under-estimated, in conventional sociological accounts concerned to view social movements in primarily class terms:

> The existing debate about citizenship therefore as a relationship between class and social membership is too narrow to deal

with the new issues of citizenship which raise legal problems concerning the political status of children, embryos, invertebrate species and inanimate forms of nature. (1986, p. 92).

2 Social movement theory

1   Most of the theorists of social movements who ally themselves with the Marxist tradition, and whom I discuss here, are more specifically structuralist Marxists. My criticisms of neo-Marxist social movement theory are thus primarily aimed at this structuralist school. It should be noted that there are quite different 'readings', and indeed theories of social movements, within Marxism which are not vulnerable to the types of criticisms levelled here, and among these are the works of E.P. Thompson and Eric Hobsbawm. I use the term 'neo-Marxism' to avoid conflating Marxism with its structuralist interpretation.
2   See, for example, Habermas, 1984; Fay, 1975; and Apel, 1980.
3   Further criticims of 'strain' models of collective action can be found in Marx and Holzer, 1977; Traugott, 1978; Melucci, 1989, chapter 1.

3 Sociological responses to the rise of new social movements

1   The essay quoted here ('The problem of violence and radical opposition') was first given as a lecture in 1967.
2   'I am supposed to have asserted that what we in America call hippies and you call *Gammler*, beatniks, are the new revolutionary class. Far be it from me to assert such a thing' (Marcuse, 1970, p. 69). The contrast between 'minority movements' and the workers' movement is not terribly satisfactory since workers themselves constitute a statistical minority, and it is difficult to think of some new social movements, in particular feminism, as minority movements.
3   Alasdair MacIntyre in his trenchant critique has noted the similarity at these points between Marcuse's views and those of modernization and convergence theorists. See MacIntyre, 1970, pp. 70–3.
4   In using the term 'naturalism' in this way I am following Touraine who defines it as 'an asocial vision of the action but also of the actor' (1983a, p. 33).
5   Touraine is not using the term 'class' here in the sense of an objective social-structural location; he means a group which has defined itself and its interests *vis-à-vis* other such groups.
6   Habermas, no less than Touraine, is concerned to differentiate progressive from regressive movements, and he suggests that only the former, and less particularistic movements, can be identified as resisting processes of inner colonialization.
7   '*Instandbesetzung*' is a pun on '*Instandsetzung*' (renovation), and implies renovation *through* occupation.

4 Varieties of ideology within the ecology movement

1　For an interesting inside account of *Die Szene* and of the *Spontaneisten*, see Huber, 1981.

2　There were between 15,000 and 20,000 such initiatives by the mid-1970s. See Mez, 1987, p. 263. For a detailed discussion of West German citizenship movements, see Mayer-Tasch, 1981.

3　A recent exception has been the opposition to the building of West Germany's first nuclear reprocessing plant at Wackersdorf in Bavaria, which has seen a number of violent clashes between police and demonstrators. The broader implications of civil disobedience have been taken up in German political theory, most notably by Habermas, 1983. Fear that the Greens' commitment to extra-parliamentary activity might lead them to endorse violent opposition led some conservative critics to argue that they were an unconstitutional force. See Stöss, 1984.

4　Grüne Liste Unwelt, Grüne Liste Schleswig-Holstein, Grüne Aktion Zukunft, Aktionsgemeinschaft Unabhängiger Deutscher and a number of smaller groups.

5　There are a number of detailed accounts of the development of the German Green Party available in English, the most comprehensive of which is Werner Hülsberg, 1988. Hülsberg writes from an eco-socialist perspective and plays down the role of citizens' initiatives. For a fundamentalist interpretation see Capra and Spretnak, 1984. There are also attempts by political scientists to identify the social base and political impact of the West German Green Party; see Müller-Rommel, 1985a and 1985b, and Bürklin, 1981 and 1987. See also E. Papadakis, 1984 and 1988 and Wolf, 1986. There is a very large literature on the Green movement and Green Party in German. Useful accounts can be found in Schäfer (ed.), 1983; Brand *et al.*, 1984 and Brand (ed.), 1985; Kluge (ed.), 1984; Roth and Rucht (eds), 1987. On the relationship between the Green Party and the SPD, see Bicherich (ed.), 1985.

6　The GAZ then tried, unsuccessfully, to establish a right-of-centre ecology party. Werner Hülsberg gives a detailed account of the struggle between Left and Right for control of the developing Green Party in West Germany, 1988, chapter 6.

7　West Germany's system of proportional representation has the modifying feature that a party must receive more than 5 per cent of the votes in federal or national elections before it can gain seats. The rationale has been that this barrier prevents the proliferation of parties, particularly those of the extreme Right.

8　Green and alternative lists, and then the Green Party, first broke the 5 per cent barrier in local and federal state (*Land*) elections in Bremen in 1979, then in Baden-Würtemberg (1979), Berlin (1981), Lower-Saxony, Hessen, and Hamburg (1982).

9 For a discussion of the West Berlin elections see *Der Spiegel*, no.6, 1989 and of the SPD/Alternative pact see the interview with Walter Momper, *Der Spiegel*, no. 12, 1989.

The growth of support for Green parties generally in Western Europe was vividly illustrated by the 1989 European election. With the exception of West Germany, where the difference was minimal, green parties have fared better in European elections than they have in national elections. The French and British cases are particularly spectacular.

10 This problem arose notably in the case of Joschka Fischer who was the first ecological politician to become a minister at *Land* level, in Hessen.

11 The cynics' reaction was neatly captured by a comment quoted in the German magazine *Der Spiegel*: '*Mein Auto fährt auch ohne Wald*' ('My car will work without the forests'). This less than laudable sentiment makes the point that resignation and cynicism are just as rational a response to impending doom as is the kind of revolution in values and life-style demanded by Bahro.

12 Tom Bottomore has pointed out to me that despite Bahro's rejection of Marxism, his more recent ecological fundamentalism retains elements of his previous fundamentalist Marxist arguments. The content, rather than the form, of the argument has changed.

13 For a detailed discussion of the arguments of Gorz and Bahro, as well as other major ecological thinkers, see Frankel, 1987. On Gorz, see Giddens, 1987b and Hirsh, 1981.

14 First published in French in 1963; English translation 1967.

15 Ironically, in these respects Gorz's arguments are not as far removed from those of Marx as he appears to believe.

16 For a critique of concepts of objective interests as determining belief, see Hindess 1986 and Scott 1988. Paul Hirst draws different conclusions from these types of consideration from those of Laclau and Mouffe. He argues that socialists must turn their attention to institutional *reform from within* the context of representative democracy. Here again, it is democracy – this time understood as greater control of, and access to, major institutions – rather than socialism, which forms the central platform of left politics: 'I have tried to show that popular democracy cannot be the sole basis of organization, that "mass" practice can be as oppressive as any other, and that the conditions of political difference and debate of policy lines can be secured only by imposing limits on central state and mass organizations' capacities' (Hirst, 1986, p. 53).

5 Movements and parties

1 The exception here is the Italian social movement theorist Alberto Melucci who recognizes the contribution of resource mobilization in explaining the 'how' of movement activity but argues, I think

rightly, that it does not tackle 'why' questions. See Melucci, 1989, p. 21.

2 There is a large literature from the perspective of resource mobilization theory. See especially McCarthy and Zald (eds.) 1979 and Gamson, 1975. For a useful review, see Jenkins, 1983. Jenkins notes that this approach emphasized the 'continuity between movement and institutionalized actions, the rationality of movement actors, the strategic problems confronted by movements, and the role of movements as agents of social change' (p. 528). These are the aspects of resource mobilization theory which I argue are its main attractions.

3 In Olson's version of rational choice theory, and in much subsequent discussion, the agent is treated as essentially self-interested. This, as I shall argue below, desocializes social actors and their actions. Later rational choice theorists have dissociated the theory from the assumption of strict egotism – see Elster 1985. Since the assumption of self-interest has been most influential in social movement theory, I shall confine the discussion to this narrower model, and primarily to the arguments of Olson and Oberschall.

4 By 'realist political analysis' I mean those approaches to politics, whether stemming from pluralism or democratic elite theory, which emphasize political integration and the limitations on political action.

5 It is worth noting in this context that Oberschall's model is the American political system and political culture with its emphasis on interest group politics.

6 This aspect is brought out clearly in a different context by Adam Przeworski who has also adopted methodological individualism. Przeworski's concern was with the conditions under which the working class adopt revolutionary action, but the arguments he develops in this context apply in part to any form of collective action which aims to bring about social change. See Przeworski, 1985, especially chapter 2.

7 There are other sociological criticisms to be made of rational choice theory. Barry Hindess has recently criticised RCT for assuming that all social actors are individual persons; see Hindess, 1988. In fact Hindess's own arguments have moved some way towards RCT in allowing the case that classes, defined exclusively in terms of social-structural location, cannot 'act'. He does nevertheless argue that institutions and organizations, for example, firms and unions, are social actors which are not reducible to individual incumbents or members.

A critique of the philosophical model of the social actor which underlies rational choice theory can be found in Hollis, 1987. A review of sociological criticisms of rational choice theory can be found in Przeworski, 1986.

8 Offe's and Wiesenthal's argument is a historical one, to the effect that dominance of instrumental action is a historically specific phenomenon the overcoming of which is a major challenge to collective organization, and which itself constitutes the creation of an alternative 'logic of collective action' – hence the title.

9 Thus Melucci contrasts traditional movements which thematize citizenship with new movements which thematize culture, identity, etc.: 'The conflicts which prompted the theoretical analysis of social movements . . . were linked historically to forms to action in which social conflict was bound up with struggle for citizenship' (1988, p. 245).

6 Social closure and political participation

1 Explanations of new social movements with reference to their specific political context rather than long term theories of social change have been developed by political scientists rather than sociologists, and the suggestions of this chapter support this approach. For examples of more context-specific, institutional and 'political' approaches to new movements see Kitschelt, 1985 and 1988; Bürklin, 1985 and 1987; Poguntke, 1987. Bürklin, 1987, interprets the rise of the German Greens as a reflection of the labour market position of their supporters. He is criticised for a too mono-causal approach (see Bürklin and Kitschelt, 1988) but such a general approach does illustrate the characteristics of an explanation in terms of closure and strategies of overcoming closure. Among more sociological commentators, Offe is farthest away from culturalist approaches, while Nedelmann, 1987, makes an interesting attempt to accomodate sociological insights with a political science approach – see below.

2 This distinction may also be expressed in terms of types of citizenship. What I have characterized as participatory demands may be defined in terms of political citizenship; other social movement themes may be characterized as social, economic or legal citizenship, etc. See Turner, 1986.

   For Castells, pluralism is 'unable to take into consideration the biases of bargaining' and has no interest in understanding the 'transformation of the social structure and its values' (1983, p. 294).

   More recently, Lafontaine has caused considerable debate within the SPD by arguing for a shortening of the working week *without* a corresponding increase in wages: in effect a lowering of pay levels. For a discussion of this line of thinking within the SPD, which has more than an elective affinity with the demands of German Greens, see *Der Spiegel*, 1988, no. 10. Lafontaine's own political position is set out in Lafontaine, 1985.

Bibliography

Alber, J. (1985), 'Modernisierung, neue Spannungslinien und die politischen Chancen der Grünen', *Politische Vierteljahresschrift*, vol. 26, no. 3, pp. 211–26.

Amery, C. (1983), 'Deutscher Konservatismus und der faschistische Graben: Versuch einer zeitgeschichtlichen Bilanz' in W. Schäfer, (ed.), op. cit., pp. 11–19.

Apel, K-O. (1980), *Towards the Transformation of Philosophy* (London: Routledge & Kegan Paul).

Bahro, R. (1977), *The Alternative in Eastern Europe* (London: Verso).

Bahro, R. (1984), *From Red to Green* (London: Verso).

Bahro, R. (1985), 'Hinein oder hinaus?' in W. Bicherich, ed., op.cit., pp. 45–75.

Banks, O. (1986), *Becoming a Feminist* (Brighton: Harvester Press).

Barrett M. and McIntosh, M. (1982), *The Anti-Social Family* (London: Verso).

Bauman, Z. (1982), *Memories of Class* (London: Routledge & Kegan Paul).

Bayard, R. (1979), *Strategies for Freedom: the Changing Pattern of Black Protest* (New York: Columbia University Press).

Bell, D. (1976), *Cultural Contradictions of Capitalism* (London: Heinemann).

Bernstein, R..J. (1979), *The Reconstruction of Social and Political Theory* (London: Methuen).

Bicherich, W. (ed.) (1985), *SPD und Grüne: Das Neue Bündnis?* (Reinbek bei Hamburg: Spiegel Verlag).

Boggs, C. (1986), *Social Movements and Political Power: Emerging Forms of Radicalism in the West* (Philadelphia: Temple University Press).

Bourdieu, P. (1985), 'The Social Space and the Genesis of Groups', *Theory and Society*, vol. 7, no. 2, pp. 723–44.

Brand, K-W., Büsser, D. and Rucht, D., (1984), *Aufbruch in eine andere Gesellschaft: Neue soziale Bewegungen in der Bundesrepublik* (Frankfurt am Main: Campus Verlag).

Brand, K–W. (ed.) (1985), *Neue soziale Bewegungen in Westeuropa und den USA: Ein internationaler Vergleich* (Frankfurt am Main: Campus Verlag).

Bürklin, W.P. (1981), 'Die Grünen und die "Neue Politik"', *Politische Vierteljahresschrift*, vol. 22, no. 4, pp. 359–82.

Bürklin, W. P. (1985), The German Greens: The post-industrial non-established and the political system', *International Political Science Review*, vol. 6, no. 4, pp. 463–81.

Bürklin, W.P. (1987), 'Governing left parties frustrating the radical non-established left: the rise and inevitable decline of the Greens', *European Sociological Review*, vol. 3, no. 2, pp. 109–26.

Capra, F. and Spretnak, C. (1984), *Green Politics: the Global Promise*: (New York: E.P. Dutton).

Castells, E. (1976), 'Theoretical propositions for an experimental study of urban social movements', in C.G. Pickvance (ed.), 1976a, op. cit., pp. 147–73.

Castells, M. (1977), *The Urban Question* (London: Edward Arnold).

Castells, M. (1978), *City, Class and Power* (London: Macmillan).

Castells, M. (1983), *The City and the Grassroots* (London: Edward Arnold).

Chandler, W.M. and Siaroff, A. (1986), 'Post-industrial politics in Germany and the origins of the Greens', *Comparative Politics*, vol. 18, no. 3, pp. 303–25.

Cohen, G.A. (1978), *Karl Marx's Theory of History: A Defence* (Oxford: Oxford University Press).

Dudek, P. (1983), 'Nationalromantischer Populismus als Zivilisations-kritik', W. Schäfer (ed.), op. cit., pp. 27–36.

Eder, K. (1982), 'New social movements?', *Telos*, no. 52, pp. 5–20.

Elias, N. (1988), 'The retreat of sociologists into the present', *Theory, Culture and Society*, vol. 4, nos. 2–3, pp. 223–48.

Elster, J. (1985), *Making Sense of Marx* (Cambridge: Cambridge University Press).

Elster, J. (ed.) (1986), *Rational Choice* (Oxford: Blackwell).

Eyerman, R. (1984), 'Social movements and social theory', *Sociology*, vol. 18, pp. 71–82.

Fay, B. (1975), *Social Theory and Political Practice* (London: Allen & Unwin).

Feher, F. and Heller A. (1983), 'From Red to Green', *Telos*, no. 59, pp. 35–44.

Fireman, B. and Gamson, W.A. (1979), 'Utilitarian logic in the resource mobilization perspective' in J.D. McCarthy and M.N. Zald, (eds), op. cit., pp. 8–44.

Fischer, J. (1985), 'Es braucht seine Zeit' in W. Bicherich (ed.), op. cit., pp. 194–200.

Frankel, B. (1987), *The Post-Industrial Utopians* (Cambridge: Polity Press).

Gallie, D. (1983), *Social Inequality and Class Radicalism in France and Britain* (Cambridge: Cambridge University Press).

Gellner, E. (1983), *Nations and Nationalism* (Oxford: Blackwell).

Geras, N. (1987), 'Post-Marxism?', *New Left Review*, no. 163, pp.

40–82.

Giddens, A. (1973), *The Class Structure of the Advanced Societies* (London: Hutchinson).

Giddens, A. (ed.) (1974), *Positivism and Sociology* (London: Heinemann).

Giddens, A. (1987a), 'Nine theses on the future of sociology', in his *Social theory and Modern Sociology* (Cambridge: Polity Press), pp. 1–22.

Giddens, A. (1987b), 'The perils of punditry: Gorz and the end of the working class' in his *Social Theory and Modern Sociology* (Cambridge: Polity Press), pp. 275–96.

Glotz, P., (ed.) (1983), *Ziviler Ungehorsam im Rechtsstaat* (Frankfurt am Main: Suhrkamp Verlag).

Goldthorpe, J.H. (1984), 'The end of convergence: corporatist and dualist tendencies in modern Western societies', in J.H. Goldthorpe (ed.), *Order and Conflict in Contemporary Capitalism*, (Oxford: Oxford University Press).

Gorz, A. (1967), *Strategy for Labour* (Boston, Mass: Beacon Press).

Gorz, A. (1982), *Farewell to the Working Class: an Essay on Post-Industrial Socialism* (London: Pluto Press).

Gorz, A. (1986), 'Kapitalistisches Konsummodell und Emanzipation: Streitgespräch zwischen André Gorz, Peter Glotz und Tilman Fischer', *Die Neue Gesellschaft*, vol. 5, pp. 388–403.

Gramsci, A. (1971), *Prison Notebooks* (London: Laurence and Wishart).

Gransow, V. and Offe, C. (1982), 'Political culture and the politics of the Social Democratic government', *Telos*, no. 53, pp. 67–80.

Gruhl, H. (1984), *Ein Planet wird geplündert* (Frankfurt am Main: Fischer Verlag).

Habermas, J. (1974), 'Rationalism Divided in Two' in A. Giddens (ed.) op cit, pp. 195–224.

Habermas, J. (1976), *Legitimation Crisis* (London: Heinemann).

Habermas, J. (1983), 'Ziviler Ungehorsam – Testfall für den demokratischen Rechtsstaat. Wider den authoritären Legalismus in der Bundesrepublik' in P. Glotz (ed.), op cit, pp. 29–53.

Habermas, J. (1987), *The Theory of Communicative Action*, Vol. 2 (Cambridge: Polity Press).

Hallensleben, A. (1984), 'Wie alles anfing: Zur Vorgeschichte der Partei Die Grünen', in T. Kluge (ed.), op. cit., pp. 154–65.

Hannigan, J.A. (1985), 'Alain Touraine, Manuel Castells and Social Movement Theory: a critical appraisal', *The Sociological Quarterly*, vol. 26, no. 4, pp. 435–54.

Harloe, M. (ed.), (1977), *Captive Cities* (London: John Wiley and Sons).

Heberle, R. (1951), *Social Movements: an introduction to political sociology* (New York: Appleton-Century-Crofts, Inc.).

Held, D. and Pollitt, C. (eds) (1986), *New Forms of Democracy* (London: Sage).

Hindess, B. (1986), '"Interests" in political analysis', in J. Law (ed.), op. cit., pp. 112–31.

Hindess, B. (1987), *Politics and Class Analysis* (Oxford: Blackwell).

Hindess, B. (1988), *Choice, Rationality and Social Theory* (London: Unwin Hyman).

Hirschman, A. (1985), *Shifting Involvements* (Oxford: Blackwell).

Hirsh, A. (1981), *The French Left* (Montréal: Black Rose Books).

Hirst, P.Q. (1986), *Law, Socialism and Democracy* (London: Allen & Unwin).

Hollis, M. (1987), *The Cunning of Reason* (Cambridge: Cambridge University Press).

Honneth, A. and Joas, H. (1988), *Social Action and Human Nature* (Cambridge: Cambridge University Press).

Huber, J. (1981), *Wer soll das alles ändern* (Berlin: Rotbuch Verlag).

Hülsberg, W. (1988), *The German Greens: a social and political profile* (London: Verso).

Inglehart, R. (1977), *The Silent Revolution: Changing Values and Political Styles among Western Publics* (Princeton: Princeton University Press).

Jenkins, J.C. (1983), 'Resource mobilization theory and the study of social movements', *Annual Review of Sociology*, vol. 9, pp. 527–53.

Katz, S and Mayer, M (1985), 'Gimme shelter: self-help housing struggles within and against the state in New York City and West Berlin', *International Journal of Urban and Regional Research*, vol. 9, no. 1, pp. 15–45.

Keane, J, (ed.) (1988), *Civil Society and the State* (London: Verso).

Kelly, P. (1984), *Fighting for Hope* (London: Chatto and Windus).

Kitschelt, H. (1985), 'Political opportunity structures and political protest: anti-nuclear movements in four democracies', *British Journal of Political Science*, vol. 16, no. 1, pp. 57–85.

Kitschelt, H (1988): 'Left-libertarian parties: explaining innovation in competitive party systems', *World Politics*, vol. 40, pp. 194–234.

Kitschelt, H and Bürklin, W.P (1988), 'Debate', *European Sociological Review*, vol. 4, no. 2, pp. 155–66.

Klein, E. (1984), *Gender Politics: From Consciousness to Mass Politics* (Cambridge, Mass: Harvard University Press).

Kluge, T. (ed.) (1984), *Grüne Politik: Der Stand einer Auseinandersetzung* (Frankfurt am Main: Fischer Verlag).

Korpi, W. (1983) *The Democratic Class Struggle* (London: Routledge & Kegan Paul).

Laclau, E. and Mouffe, C. (1985), *Hegemony and Socialist Strategy: Towards a Radical Democratic Politics* (London: Verso).

Lafontaine, O. (1985), *Der andere Fortschritt* (Hamburg: Hoffmann und Campe Verlag).

Lash, S. and Urry, J. (1987), *The End of Organized Capitalism* (Cambridge: Polity).

Law, J. (ed.) (1986), *Power, Action and Belief: a new sociology of knowledge*, Sociological Review Monograph 32 (London: Routledge & Kegan Paul).

Lovenduski, J. (1986), *Women and European Politics: Contemporary Feminism and Public Policy* (Brighton: Wheatsheaf Books).

Lowe, S. (1986), *Urban Social Movements: The City After Castells* (London: Macmillan).

Lukács, G. (1971), *History and Class Consciousness* (London: Merlin).

MacIntyre, A. (1970), *Marcuse* (London: Fontana).

Maier, C.S. (ed.) (1987), *Changing Boundaries of the Political* (Cambridge: Cambridge University Press).

Marable, M. (1985) *Black American Politics* (London: Verso).

Marcuse, H. (1969), 'Revolution aus Ekel', *Der Spiegel*, vol. 23, no. 31, pp. 103–6.

Marcuse, H. (1970), *Five Lectures: Psychoanalysis, Politics and Utopia*, translated J.J. Shapiro and S.M. Weber (London: Allen Lane, the Penguin Press).

Marx, J.H. and Holzner, B. (1977), 'The Social Construction of Strain and Ideological Models of Grievance in Contemporary Movements', *Pacific Sociological Review*, vol. 20, no. 3, pp. 411–37.

Mayer-Tasch, P.C. (1981), *Die Bürgerinitiativbewegung*, 2nd edn (Reinbek bei Hamburg: Rowohlt).

McCarthy, J.D and Zald, M.N. (eds) (1979), *The Dynamics of Social Movements* (Cambridge, Mass: Winthrop Publishers, Inc.).

McCarthy, T. (1978), *The Critical Theory of Jürgen Habermas* (London: Hutchinson).

Meehan, E. M. (1985), *Women's Rights at Work: Campaigns and Policy in Britain and the United States* (London: Macmillan).

Meier, A. (1988), 'The peace movement: some questions concerning its social nature and structure', *International Sociology*, vol. 3, no. 1, pp. 77–87.

Melucci, A. (1980), 'The new social movements: a theoretical approach', *Social Science Information*, vol. 19, no. 2, pp. 199–226.

Melucci, A. (1981), Ten hypotheses for the analysis of new movements', in D. Pinto, (ed.), op. cit., pp. 173–94.

Melucci, A. (1984), 'An end to social movements?', *Social Science Information*, vol. 23, no. 4/5, pp. 819–35.

Melucci, A (1988), 'Social movements and the democratization of everyday life', in J. Keane (ed.) op. cit., pp. 245–60.

Melucci, A (1989), *Nomads of the Present* (London: Radius).

Mewes, H. (1983), 'The West German Green Party', *New German Critique*, vol. 28, pp. 51–85.

Mez, L. (1987), 'Von den Bürgerinitiativen zu den Grünen', in R. Roth and D. Rucht (eds), op. cit., pp. 263–76.

Mills, C. Wright (1970) [1959], *The Sociological Imagination* (London: Penguin).

Morris, A.D. (1984), *The Origins of the Civil Rights Movement: Black Communities Organizing for Change* (New York: Free Press).

Müller-Rommel, F. (1985a), 'Social movements and the Greens: the new internal politics in Germany', *European Journal of Political Research*, vol. 13, pp. 53–67.

Müller-Rommel, F. (1985b), 'The Greens in West Germany: similar but different', *International Political Science Review*, vol. 6, no. 4, pp. 483–99.

Nedelmann, B. (1984), 'New political movements and changes in processes of intermediation', *Social Science Information*, vol. 23, no. 6., pp. 1,029–48.

Nedelmann, B. (1987), 'Individuals and parties: changes in processes of political mobilization', *European Sociological Review*, vol. 3, no. 3, pp. 181–202.

Nelles, W. (1984), 'Kollektive Identität und politisches Handeln in neuen sozialen Bewegungen', *Politische Vierteljahreschrift*, vol. 25, no. 4, pp. 425–40.

Oberschall, A. (1973), *Social Conflict and Social Movement* (Englewood Cliffs: Prentice Hall).

Offe, C. (1980), 'Am Staat vorbei? Krise der Parteien und neue soziale Bewegungen', *Das Argument*, vol. 22, no. 124, pp. 809–21.

Offe, C. and Wiesenthal, H. (1985), 'Two logics of collective action', in C. Offe *Disorganized Capitalism* (Cambridge: Polity Press).

Offe, C. (1987), 'Changing boundaries of institutional politics: social movements since the 1960s', in C.S. Maier, (ed.), op.cit., pp. 63–106.

Olson, M. (1965), *The Logic of Collective Action* (Harvard: Harvard University Press).

Opp, K-D. (1986), 'Soft incentives and collective action: participation in the anti-nuclear movement', *British Journal of Political Science*, vol. 16, pp. 87–112.

Papadakis, E. (1984), *The Green Movement in West Germany* (London: Croom Helm).

Papadakis, E. (1988), 'Social movements, self-limiting radicalism and the Green Party in West Germany', *Sociology*, vol. 22, no. 3, pp. 433–54.

Parkin, F. (1979) *Marxism and Class Theory: a Bourgeois Critique* (London: Tavistock).

Pelinka, A. (1980), 'Zustand und Alternativen des politischen Systems', *Österreichische Zeitschrift für Politikwissenschaft*, vol. 1, pp. 25–32.

Pelinka, A. (1987), 'Austrian social partnership: stability versus innovation, *West European Politics*, vol. 10, no. 1, pp. 63–76.

Pickvance, C.G. (ed.) (1976a), *Urban Sociology: Critical Essays* (London: Tavistock).
Pickvance, C.G. (1976b), 'On the study of urban social movements' in C.G. Pickvance, (ed.) op. cit., pp. 198–218.
Pickvance, C.G. (1977), 'From "social base" to "social force": some analytical issues in the study of urban protest' in M. Harloe (ed.), op. cit.
Pinto, D. (ed.) (1981), *Contemporary Italian Sociology* (Cambridge: Cambridge University Press).
Piven, F.F. and Cloward, R.A. (1977), *Poor People's Movements: Why they Succeed, How they Fail* (New York: Vintage Books).
Poguntke, T (1987), 'New politics and party systems', *West European Politics*, vol. 10, pp. 76–88.
Przeworski, A. (1985), *Capitalism and Social Democracy* (Cambridge: Cambridge University Press).
Przeworski, A. (1986), 'Marxism and rational choice', *Politics and Society*, vol. 14, no. 4, pp. 397–409.

Reynaud, J-D. and Bourdieu, P. (1974), 'Is a sociology of action possible?', in A. Giddens (ed.), op. cit., pp. 110–114.
Roth, R. and Rucht, D. (eds) (1987), *Neue soziale Bewegungen in der Bundesrepublik Deutschland* (Bonn: Bundeszentrale für politische Bildung).
Rowbotham, S., Segal, L. and Wainwright H., (eds) (1979), *Beyond the Fragments: Feminism and the Meaning of Socialism* (London: The Merlin Press).
Rowbotham, S. (1979), 'The Women's Movement and Organizing for Socialism', in Rowbotham *et al*, (eds) op. cit., pp. 21–157.
Rustin, B. (1976), *Strategies for Freedom: the Changing Pattern of Black Protest* (New York: Columbia University Press).

Sassoon, J. (1984), 'Ideology, symbolic action and ritual in social movements: the effect on organizational forms', *Social Science Information*, vol. 23, no. 4/5, pp. 861–73.
Saunders, P. (1981), *Social Theory and the Urban Question* (London: Hutchinson).
Schäfer, W. (ed.) (1983), *Neue Soziale Bewegungen: konservativer Aufbruch in buntem Gewand?* (Frankfurt am Main: Fischer Verlag).
Schily, O. (1985), 'Vor unvergleichlichen Möglichkeiten', in W. Bicherich, (ed.), op. cit., pp. 275–9.
Schmitter, P.C. (1979), 'Modes of interest intermediation and models of societal change in Western Europe', in P.C. Schmitter and G. Lehmbruck (eds) op. cit.
Schmitter, P.C. and Lehmbruck G. (eds) (1979), *Trends Towards Corporatist Intermediation* (Beverly Hills: Sage).
Scott, A. (1988), 'Imputing beliefs: a controversy in the sociology of knowledge', *Sociological Review*, vol. 36, no. 1, pp. 31–56.

Sen, A. (1982), 'Rational fools: a critique of the behaviourial foundation of economic theory', in A. Sen *Choice, Welfare and Measurement* (Oxford: Blackwell).

Smelser, N. (1962), *Theories of Collective Behaviour* (London: Routledge & Kegan Paul).

Der Spiegel (1988), no. 6, pp. 25–31.

Der Spiegel (1989), no. 6, pp. 25–7 and no. 12, pp. 28–30.

Streeck, W. and Schmitter, P.C. (eds) (1985), 'Community, market, state and association?' in W. Streeck and P.C Schmitter (eds) *Private Interest Government* (Beverly Hills: Sage).

Stöss, R. (1984), 'Sollen die Grünen verboten werden? Zur Kritik konservativer Staatsrechtslehrer an der Verfassungsmässigkeit der Grünen/Alternativen', *Politische Vierteljahresschrift*, vol. 25, no. 4, pp. 403–24.

Touraine, A. (1971), *The Post-Industrial Society – Tomorrow's Social History: Classes, Conflicts and Culture in the Programmed Society* (New York: Random House).

Touraine, A. (1974), 'Towards a sociology of action', in A. Giddens (ed.), op. cit., pp. 75–100.

Touraine, A. (1981), *The Voice and the Eye: an Analysis of Social Movements* (Cambridge: Cambridge University Press).

Touraine, A., Hegedus, Z. and Wieviorka, M. (1983a), *Anti-Nuclear Protest: the Opposition to Nuclear Energy in France* (Cambridge: Cambridge University Press).

Touraine, A., Dubet, F., Wieviorka, M. and Strzeleck, J. (1983b), *Solidarity: Poland 1980–81* (Cambridge: Cambridge University Press).

Traugott, M. (1978), 'Reconceiving social movements', *Social Problems*, vol. 26, no. 1, pp. 38–49.

Turner. B.S. (1986), *Citizenship and Capitalism: The Debate Over Reformism* (London: Allen & Unwin).

Wainwright, H. (1979), 'Introduction' to Rowbotham *et al.*, op. cit., pp. 1–21.

Ware, A. (1986), 'Political parties', in D. Held and C. Pollitt (eds), op. cit., pp. 110–34.

Winch, P. (1958), *The Idea of a Social Science* (London: Routledge & Kegan Paul).

Wood, E.M. (1986), *The Retreat From Class: A New 'True' Socialism* (London: Verso).

Wolf, O. (1986), 'Eco-socialist transition on the threshold of the twenty-first century', *New Left Review*, no. 158, pp. 32–42.

Index